Information Management
and Organizational Change
in Higher Education

Supplements to Computers in Libraries

Information Management and Organizational Change in Higher Education

The Impact on Academic Libraries

Edited by Gary M. Pitkin

Meckler

Westport • London

Library of Congress Cataloging-in-Publication Data

Information management and organizational change in higher education :
   the impact on academic libraries / edited by Gary M. Pitkin.
       p. cm. -- (Supplements to Computers in libraries ; 59)
   Expanded versions of papers presented during a full-day seminar
conducted during the Computers in Libraries Annual Conference held
in Washington, D. C., on March 6, 1992.
   Includes index.
   ISBN 0-88736-842-5 : $
1. Libraries, University and college--Automation--Management-
-Congresses. 2. Education, Higher--Data processing--Congresses.
3. Information technology--Management--Congresses. 4. Libraries and
education--Congresses. 5. Organizational change--Congresses.
I. Pitkin, Gary M., 1947-   . II. Series.
Z675.U5157 1992
027.70285--dc20   92-17535
                                                             CIP

British Library Cataloguing-in-Publication Data

Information Management and Organizational
Change in Higher Education: Impact on
Academic Libraries
   I. Pitkin, Gary M.
   027.7

ISBN 0-88736-842-5

Copyright © 1992 Meckler Publishing. All rights reserved. No part of
this publication may be reproduced in any form by any means without prior
written permission from the publisher, except by a reviewer who may quote
brief passages in review.

Meckler Publishing, the publishing division of Meckler Corporation,
   11 Ferry Lane West, Westport, CT 06880.
Meckler Ltd., Artillery House, Artillery Row, London SW1P 1RT, U.K.

Printed on acid free paper.
Printed and bound in the United States of America.

Contents

Preface

Information management and associated technologies are a driving force of organizational change in higher education. Institutions are emulating the business sector in the transformation from hierarchically-based to network-based environments. The academic library can be either a proactive participant or a reactive victim of organizational change. The purpose of this monograph is to emphasize the former through the examination of the transformation process and the political, managerial, service, and technological issues that must be addressed by the academic library.

The chapters that follow are "based" on papers presented during a full-day seminar entitled "Information Management and Organizational Change in Higher Education: The Impact on Academic Libraries" conducted during the Computers in Libraries Annual Conference held in Washington, D.C., on March 6, 1992. The chapters do not constitute a simple republication of the presentations. The conference papers described themes and concepts; the chapters are more focused and expand greatly on the concepts and arguments originally presented.

For the purposes of discussing information management and organizational change in higher education, the chapters are arranged in three sections, each expanding upon information and concepts provided in the former sections. The initial chapter serves as an introduction. Comprising the first section, this chapter provides definitions for concepts that will be utilized throughout the subsequent sections. The definitions are presented through historical perspectives of development and include information, the management of information, the information revolution, the process of transformation, and the chief information officer concept.

The second section, "Information Management in Higher Education," is a set of three chapters that provide a transition from the concepts presented in the first chapter to the impact of information management and organizational change on the academic library. These three chapters focus on organizational change now occurring in higher education and the role that information management is playing in that "transformation." The process of transformation is clarified as it relates specifically to postsecondary institutions. The role of the Chief Information Officer in the transformation process is also presented. The progression from information management to transformation to the Chief Information Officer to the academic library culminates with the final chapter in this section.

The third section, "The Impact on the Academic Library," addresses the political, managerial, service, and technological impacts of the concepts discussed in the previous sections. As an information-oriented entity within the postsecondary organization, the effects of information management, transformation, and the role of the Chief Information Officer can be substantial. These elements are creating organizational change, and the academic library will be involved. The three chapters in this section focus on the level of involvement and the impact on the library as an organization.

Organizational change is taking place in higher education. This monograph will help librarians and others understand the concepts that constitute this change and anticipate the impact of those concepts.

Gary M. Pitkin

I. INTRODUCTION

Definitions and Perspectives

Gary M. Pitkin

The purpose of this introductory chapter is to set the stage for the chapters that follow, and their discussion of information management, organizational change, and the impact on academic libraries. These chapters have titles that contain the terms "information management," "chief information officer," and "transformation."

These concepts are beginning to affect organizational change in higher education. Reasons, processes, and results are described in subsequent chapters. To help build a context for these chapters and the major concepts involved, definitions and perspectives on those terms follow.

An Historical Perspective: Information Management and the Chief Information Officer

The *Oxford English Dictionary* defines information as the "action of informing; formation or moulding of the mind or character, training, instruction, teaching; communication of instructive knowledge."[1] This definition is intrinsic to the role and mission of higher education in society in that through the "communication of instructive knowledge" institutions mould the minds of students, provide "training, instruction, teaching," and generally engage in the "action of informing."

Indeed, the institutions that comprise higher education have the obligation to provide necessary information to students, faculty, administrators, and staff. This has always been the case; but the so-called "information explosion" or "information revolution" of the 1980s and 1990s has caused such a proliferation of information that managing it has become difficult and confusing. The "information revolution" is defined in the *Oxford English Dictionary* as "the increase in the availability of information and the changes in the ways it is stored and disseminated that have occurred through the use of computers."[2]

The realization of the "information age" has been reached through a progression of technological eras or stages. Those eras and stages are conceptualized by Marchand, Rockart, and Ryland and are summarized in Table 1.[3, 4, 5] Marchand and Rockart established their descriptions from the per-

1

Business Sector		Higher Education
Marchand (1985)	Rockart (1988)	Ryland (1989)
Stage 1 Physical Control (1900-1950s)	The Accounting Era (1950s-early 1960s)	The Automated Data Processing Era (1950s-mid 1960s)
Stage 2 Management of Automated Technology (1960s-mid 1970s)	The Operational Era (early 1960s-late 1970s)	The Era of Integration (mid 1960s-late 1970s)
Stage 3 Information Resources Management (mid 1970s-1980s)	The Information Era (late 1970s-early 1980s)	The Individual Computing Era (late 1970s)
Stage 4 Knowledge Management (late 1980s-1990s)	The Wired Society (early 1980s)	

Table 1. Historical perspectives of computing.

spective of the business sector, while Ryland's time periods depict computing history in higher education.

Although the three authors use different titles, they agree conceptually on the evolutionary events leading to the current information revolution. Until the early to mid 1960s, computing was really mechanization. Data were controlled through the use of typewriters, telephones, tabulating machines, and microfilm.[6] Computers, which were sophisticated tabulating machines, were used to process mathematical data in a batch environment using punched cards.[7] Applications were limited to accounting functions such as payroll and invoice processing.[8]

From the early to mid 1960s through the mid to late 1970s, the management of information expanded through the development of photocopy machines, enhancements to voice communications, and the development of computers that were more than number-crunchers.[9] Ryland describes this time period as the era during which computers made the transition from handling data for recordkeeping purposes to manipulating data to aid the decision-making process. This was the beginning of the development of management information systems.[10]

From the mid to late 1970s to the mid 1980s, the functionality of computers increased dramatically. Information management, rather than the manipulation of simple data through data management, became the norm through the use of minicomputers, microcomputers, personal computers, and integrated voice and data networks. This created a distributed rather than a centralized computing environment, which allowed computerized information processing to take place in functional departments and on desktops rather than through a mainframe at a central location.[11] Individuals rather than centralized system managers processed information through the functions of word processing, electronic mail, time management, and personal computing.[12]

Since the mid 1980s, we have entered what Rockart calls "the wired society," which is related to what Marchand refers to as "knowledge management."[13, 14] The wired society refers to the current ability of computers and telecommunications technology to allow online, interactive communication between and among departments and individuals. Information is shared and communicated as it is developed. Marchand contends that the sophistication of current technology allows the sharing of knowledge, not just information. He defines knowledge management as "the ability to search for, have insight into, analyze and synthesize questions, problems and alternatives to resolve or solve significant needs, concerns and interests."[15] Ryland, in describing the history of computing in higher education, complements Marchand's definition by referring to the current time period as an era of information manipulation and not simply of information management.[16]

During the time periods described by Marchand, Rockart, and Ryland, the technology used to manage information changed with each succeeding era. The organizational structures put in place by business and higher education also changed with each succeeding era and were direct responses to the increasing abilities of new technology and the increasing applications of individuals.

Until the late 1970s, computerized activities and the associated hardware were centralized. Information managers with such variant titles as Electronic Data Processing Manager, Information Systems Manager/Director, or Computer Center Manager/Director supervised an isolated staff that made all the data-processing decisions.[17] This included developing criteria for the input of data and the formats for the resulting administrative tools.

The advent of personal computers in the late 1970s and 1980s and the ability of individuals to use them to create personal designs of information and to dictate output formats, led to a decentralization of computing.[18] Users were not only employing personal computers to create their own data for a particular purpose, they were using telecommunications systems to send information to each other. Information technology was no longer a centralized service in an isolated department provided to the organization. Information technology was being incorporated into the everyday work life of the individual. Managers of departments purchased their own software and hardware, developed their own protocols, purchased their own local area networks, and designed or purchased electronic mail systems to allow persons in their areas to communicate with each other.

Distributed computing and all of its advantages for the end-user have created what Battin calls a paradox. "The paradox of information technology is that it makes possible an unprecedented decentralization of technical power to individual option while at the same time it requires a globally coordinated infrastructure to permit the effective individual exercise of that power."[19]

In the early 1980s, businesses began to implement decentralized environments that allowed a great deal of latitude to the individual user. Battin's paradox was soon realized, however, because department managers were purchasing systems independently from other departments.[20] The result was a form of chaos: interdepartmental computing was not possible; strategic objectives for computing were nonexistent; computing was department-controlled and not business-controlled. In short, it was out of control. A lot of money was being spent on systems that were incompatible with each other and would eventually have to be replaced.

The business sector responded to this problem by creating the position of Chief Information Officer (CIO). As described by Synnott, the title of Chief Information Officer is generic and describes a particular role and function. Actual titles for the position vary among companies, but the most common are Director of Information Resources Management, Vice President of Corporate Systems, and Senior Vice President of Information Systems.[21]

In addressing the paradox of the advantages of decentralized computing and the resultant requirement of a strong infrastructure, the Chief Information Officer was assigned all policy and coordination responsibility for information management.[22] The Chief Information Officer's role is very different from that of the computer manager of the past. Chief Information Officers are not computer gurus. Instead, as described by Synnott, "The new breed of information managers, the CIOs, are businessmen first, managers second, and technologists third."[23]

Higher education has experienced the same paradox of decentralized computing as the business sector. This parallel is made by Robinson, Augustson, Ryland, Penrod and Dolence, and Woodsworth. Decentralization in higher education was caused by the same advances in technology and the same proliferation of information that affected the business sector, but the resulting problems are unique because of higher education's teaching function and its traditional organizational separation of information technologies between academic and administrative functions.[24, 25, 26, 27, 28]

In many institutions of higher education, especially the larger research-oriented universities, administrative computing and academic computing have been historically separate. This separation was based on function. Administrative computing handled basic recordkeeping and data management functions, including accounting, payroll, student records, enrollment figures, and personnel information.[29,30] This type of computing is similar to that of the business sector because emphasis was on automating labor-intensive administrative responsibilities. Computing was seen as a way to minimize clerical functions and costs, including salaries, associated with those functions.[31]

In contrast, academic computing supports the learning environment, not the business environment, of the higher education institution. This has been accomplished through establishing and maintaining student computer rooms; training for faculty on microcomputer applications; implementing and maintaining local, regional, national, and international communication networks; and helping faculty design and use software for instructional purposes.[32]

Because of these functional differences, administrative and academic computing have been historically separate. This is true in terms of administrative locus and hardware use. As in the business sector, advances in information technology and the proliferation of information are influencing substantial changes.

> In a distributed computing environment, the need to access different kinds of information in a seamless fashion makes it imperative that these two areas work harmoniously. Administrative users, for example, require the same kinds of word-processing and other productivity tools as do faculty. Faculty need access to administrative databases of many kinds to support student advising and the processing of grants. And at a departmental level, the boundaries between "academic" and "administrative" computing may be hard to discern. Computing organizations may see a clear difference between what is academic computing and what is administrative computing, but to a growing number of users, such distinctions are increasingly meaningless and frustrating.[33]

The combining of functionality between administrative and academic computing caused by technology and access to information dictates coordinated planning and systems integration.[34] According to Vaught, this is causing the current trend of administrative and academic computing being reunited under one administrative locus sharing a common hardware platform.[35]

Administrative and academic computing are being systematically reintegrated because of what Hawkins refers to as the need to coordinate and control planning and spending for the benefit of the entire institution.[36] This is the same reasoning that caused the creation of the Chief Information Officer position in the business sector. But there is an organizational difference. In higher education, there are separate administrative divisions, in addition to administrative and academic computing, for telecommunications, office automation, mail services, reproduction services, printing, institutional research, television services, audio-visual services, library services, and instructional development.[37] While reporting mechanisms vary among institutions, those units traditionally set their own goals and have autonomous latitude with budgeting and staffing. In addition, they are uncoordinated as a group in planning and function as some report to the academic side of the institution, some to the administrative side, and some to student affairs.

All of these entities are involved in information management, and they employ information technology. Even more important within this context, they are very expensive units in terms of operational, capital, and personnel budgets. The decentralized capability of personal computers, voice/data networks, and online databases is causing institutional administrators to question the role and mission of these units. In addition, questions are being raised about the feasibility of merging these units under one administrative branch.

As a result, some institutions have taken steps to centralize all areas involved with managing information. Penrod states that it is imperative for higher education to implement centralized planning and coordinate all aspects of information technology.[38] Woodsworth states that many institutions see these units as competing to provide the same services.[39] The result is an unnecessary and wasteful duplication of effort, staff, and financial resources.[40]

In an effort to resolve this unproductive situation, institutions have followed the example set by the business sector. In order to effectively address the decentralization paradox described earlier by Battin, higher education has also created the Chief Information Officer position. Penrod, Dolence, and Douglas (1990) identify three types of Chief Information Officers in higher education:

1. *Vice President*. Generally, this title is Vice President for Information Services, Vice President for Information Resources, or Vice President for Computing Services. The position reports directly to the president/ chancellor of the institution, is an executive officer, sets policy for the division, and is instrumental in setting policy for the university. The position has direct contact with other executive officers, namely the vice presidents and deans, in the decision-making process.

2. *Associate Vice President*. Generally, this title is Associate Vice President for Information Services or Associate Vice President for Information Resources. This position reports directly to the provost or academic vice president and may or may not function as an executive officer of the institution. The position does have policy authority over most information service units, with the library and media services as possible exceptions. The position does have direct contact with the vice presidents and deans.

3. *Director*. Generally, this title is Director of Computing, Director of Computing Services, or Director of Information Services. This position re-

ports to a vice president or associate vice president, is not an executive officer, and has limited policy authority. The Director has the authority to set policy for academic and administrative computing but not for other providers of
information services. In some cases, there may be separate directors for academic and administrative computing. This position has little contact with vice
presidents and deans.[41]

Recent studies conducted by Penrod, Dolence, and Douglas and
Woodsworth reveal that the number of higher education institutions that have
implemented either the first or second category of Chief Information Officer
has doubled every two years since 1986.[42, 43] By the end of 1989, one-third
of the higher education institutions in the nation either had or were searching
for a Chief Information Officer.[44] Hawkins predicts that the number of positions will increase by another 20 percent by 1993.[45] The third category, that
of Director, is being systematically eliminated in favor of individuals who are
more involved with planning and setting institutional policy than those who
are technically oriented.

The Chief Information Officer Defined

The Chief Information Officer position is described above as evolving
through historical eras or stages in concert with the evolution of the technology employed to manage information. These historical periods progressed
from an initial era of mechanization and number-crunching to the current environment that caused Battin's paradox of "an unprecedented decentralization
of technical power to individual option while at the same time [requiring] a
globally coordinated infrastructure to permit the effective individual exercise
of that power."[46]

Synnott recognized the paradox and the changing skills needed to
manage the decentralized environment and compared those skills to previous
eras by stating that:

> The CIO concept has piqued widespread interest because
> business and information managers alike see the change
> from the Computer Era to the Information Era, understand
> that technology is becoming vital and persuasive to busi-
> ness, and recognize that a new brand of leadership is need-
> ed to manage increasingly decentralized and complex infor-
> mation resources. The skills needed to manage the
> centralized data processing shop of the past are very differ-
> ent skills from those necessary to manage distributed infor-
> mation resources. Technical skills have to be supplemented
> with solid business, organizational, political, managerial,

and interpersonal skills to integrate business and technology effectively.[47]

The nature of the position employed to manage information and the associated technology changed as dramatically as the time periods with which they were associated. The analysis provided in Table 2 illustrates how the position changed in conjunction with the historical periods named by Ryland.[48]

Ryland's analysis of the evolution of the information manager from data processor to Chief Information Officer is supported by Penrod and Dolence and Rockart.[49, 50] Penrod and Dolence describe the function of the information manager as evolving from having to convince co-workers of the utility of information systems to working with them to implement demanded systems; from integrating all information functions into a centralized unit to decentralizing them throughout the organization; from employing technology to carry out specific tasks to employing technology to accomplish organization-wide strategic goals; from supervising a staff of implementers to supervising a staff of designers and consultants; and from managing a single unit responsible for information management to developing a participatory approach with all organization managers to manage information.[51] Rockart addresses the evolution from data processor to Chief Information Officer by distinguishing between traditional and new functions. The former are described as responsibility for the technical design of computer applications, programming, managing specific projects and operations, and supervising a staff that consults with and educates users on specific applications.[52]

The new functions, that Rockart cites for implementation in the late 1980s and early 1990s, are the result of a decentralized computing environment and the necessity of a centralized infrastructure lead by a Chief Information Officer. These functions are the design of complex systems to facilitate the accomplishment of the organizational mission and the development and maintenance of an infrastructure that deals with all elements of information technology, that is, computers, networks, software, data. This involves educating all line managers as to the importance and capabilities of information systems, and educating all information management staff as to organization-wide goals, that is, the "business" of the organization, as opposed to simple task-orientation. It also involves operating in a proactive rather than a reactive fashion to plan for and assess information management applications throughout the organization.[53] Rockart summarizes his evolutionary description by stating that:

> The role of the information system executive has . . . expanded. He or she is now a business executive—increasingly responsible for providing the line [department

managers] with knowledge about applicable technology and with the tools and infrastructure that allow development and implementation of innovative business systems.[54]

Information Eras and Manager Responsibility Adapted from Ryland

	Automated Data Processing Era (1950s-Mid 1960s)	Era of Integration (Mid 1960s-Late 1970s)	Individual Computing Era (late 1970s-)
Characteristics of the era	−computing was really mechanization −computers were sophisticated tabulating machines −applications were limited to mathematical computations such as accounting functions	−computers were more sophisticated --applications expanded from simple tabulation to the manipulation of data for decision-making purposes --databases were created and administered for institutional and interdepartmental use	--decentralization of computing resources from a centralized information unit to the end user −implementation of microcomputers for individualized computing, including word processing −manipulation of information, not simply managing information
Title and working relationships of the information manager	Automated Data Processing Manager −reported to a vice-president or chief financial officer --responsible for systems design and operation, programming, and formatting data --information management was centralized to control all aspects of computing	Information Systems Manager −reported to a vice-president −began to work with users to design data for decision-making purposes --because applications were becoming institution-wide, a knowledge of the business became important	Chief Information Officer --an executive-level position --decentralization required a thorough understanding of the business and departmental interrelationships became the first priority --responsible for strategic planning at the organization-wide level --the end-user environment required a participatory approach to managing information

Table 2.

In this statement, Rockart refers to the Chief Information Officer as an information systems executive and as a business executive. Unlike the data processing manager, the Chief Information Officer is responsible for the employment of information management in meeting the organization's overall goals and mission. Unlike the data processing manager, the Chief Information Officer is instrumental in strategic planning for the entire organization and consequently works very closely with the top management of the organization. The information manager is no longer in charge of an isolated unit, but is a business executive responsible, with other executives, for the success of the organization as a whole.

This concept of the CIO as a top-level executive has much support. Synnott describes the position as "the highest ranking executive with primary responsibility for information management."[55] Gantz states that the CIO functions at the executive level of the organization.[56] Turner refers to the Chief Information Officer as the executive in charge of long-range planning and technology.[57] Augustson describes the CIO as an "executive-level person who has responsibility for planning for information technology initiatives."[58] Dillman and Hicks refer to the position as senior-level management.[59]

According to Penrod, Dolence, and Douglas, the first thorough description of the Chief Information Officer concept was made by Synnott and Gruber.[60] Woodsworth affirmed this by stating that Synnott and Gruber provide "the most comprehensive description of the role and responsibilities of the chief information officer."[61] This description was, however, hypothetical. They were calling for the implementation of the Chief Information Officer concept throughout the corporate world and described this new position in relationship to electronic data processing (EDP) in the following way:

> . . . No longer technical back shop wizards running arcane machines in support of a company's clerical record keeping and/or transaction based systems, today's new breed of EDP managers are moving out of the back shop and into business manager roles. They are taking on new and broader responsibilities and repositioning EDP in the organization so as to be more influential, more participatory, and more responsive to users' business systems needs as well as to executive information needs. Those who are succeeding in this transition are migrating from being the data processors of the past to being the information managers of the future.
>
> . . . The CIO of the firm will be responsible for establishing corporate information policies, standards, and procedures for information resource management in the corpo-

ration and will identify, coalesce, and manage information as a resource. Because information is a necessary and important ingredient in corporate and business planning, decision support systems, and control activities, the CIO will necessarily be involved in these activities with senior managers throughout the firm . . . . The CIO in the corporate organization structure should be able to provide centralized management and control over information processing and utilization, even though it may be distributed geographically and functionally throughout the organization.

. . . The CIO is a concept whose time has come. Leading-edge information managers will gradually evolve into that role during the 1980s as they integrate technology more effectively with user and senior management business and information needs . . . . As we move into the information age of the 1980s, the new breed of information managers will become integrated into the businesses they serve by working more closely with users and senior management in solving their problems and serving their needs, will marshall their information resources for the solution of business problems and in support of management, and will move up the corporate ladder as their firms' chief information officers.[62]

For the Chief Information Officer to be effective in this executive role, he or she will serve the organization in the capacities of strategic planner, change agent, information manager, proactivist, business manager, politician, integrator, information controller, staff professional, manager, and futurist.[63] Responsibilities for each role are as follows:

1. *Strategic Planner*. Not only will the CIO be responsible for planning system strategies, he or she will be responsible for incorporating information management and technology into all aspects of the strategic planning process and into solving problems throughout the corporate structure. The CIO is a key component of the corporate planning team.

2. *Change Agent*. The change process is greatly influenced by rapid enhancements to computer technology and the resultant proliferation of information. The ability to manage information for the purpose of specific functions influences change within departments and throughout the entire organization. The CIO must control this influence on change by communicating with managers and executives so that change is anticipated and planned. CIOs must, at the same time, positively influence change by educating managers and executives as to the abilities of information management.

3. *Information Manager*. The CIO will serve the organization by supporting decentralized computing while being certain that all processes needed for success are incorporated into a centralized management infrastructure. In this way, the CIO establishes a mechanism whereby all sectors of the organization receive services and information. It also assures the organization that information technology will be employed to allow communication within and among all departments for the benefit of the total organization.

4. *Proactivist*. The CIO must be actively involved, through his or her own initiative, in the application of information management and technology to business processes. The CIO must aggressively make department managers and corporate leadership fully aware of the importance of information management to the mission of the organization. Opportunities to employ information systems to solve problems and consequently to affect the bottom line must be proactively pursued. The CIO who only reacts to applications will be ineffective.

5. *Business Manager*. The role of the CIO will be to effectively employ information management for the benefit of the corporation. In the current decentralized environment, this can only be accomplished if the CIO has a thorough knowledge of the business of the organization and a complete understanding of the responsibilities and functionality of all units. The CIO will develop and implement applications that cross departmental and functional lines. The CIO will have to combine a decentralized environment with business needs and information technology. This can be accomplished only if the CIO is a businessman first and a technician second.

6. *Politician*. Because the CIO must operate at a corporate-wide interdepartmental level, he or she must have the ability to recognize and deal positively with organizational politics. This requires not only the ability to recognize power bases but to also create them for the benefit of information management use throughout the organization. Political strength also requires excellent communication and interpersonal skills. It also requires the ability to become aware of personal needs and to be sensitive to those needs. Through the daily application of these skills, the CIO will gain the respect of information users and corporate management and will consequently further the information management agenda.

7. *Integrator*. A major function of the CIO will be to integrate all elements of information technology into a coordinated and fully integrated information structure. This will involve integrating the functionality of computers, telecommunications, and software into a total corporate system that will serve the needs of all managers and staff. This will involve the CIO's proactive attitude and political skills to gain the support of all corporate constituencies, because of the effect that integration will have on distributed systems, office automation, and the electronic delivery of information.

8. *Information Controller*. The CIO will control information in a decentralized environment by maintaining a centralized infrastructure for the management of information. While hardware, software, and applications are distributed throughout the organization, the CIO controls that decentralization by managing information as a corporate resource shared at the departmental level. Every application employed by every department is dependent on that centralized source. This dependence is part of the integration role of the CIO and is effective because of the roles listed above.

9. *Staff Professional*. By serving as an executive in a staff position, the CIO is responsible for providing the organization with information management applications that support the decision-making process. In this role, again using the skills cited above, the CIO will provide the organization with information-based and research-based systems, guidance on application and purchase, implementation scenarios for successful implementation of purchased systems, and planning documents for future applications and purchases.

10. *Manager*. As an executive officer, the CIO, in addition to managing information, manages what all other executives manage: people, budgets, capital resources, inter- and intra-departmental relationships, projects, and communications. He or she must have the organizational skills required of any manager.

11. *Futurist*. As an information manager, the CIO must be cognizant of advances in information technology and their application to information management. More precisely, he or she must be aware at all times of new developments and their applicability to the organization. As a corporate executive and business manager, the CIO must be constantly aware of business trends and their effect on the organization. The CIO must, unlike the other executives, combine trends in information management with trends in business to be able to incorporate the use of information management in the future of the organization.

The roles identified by Synnott and Gruber are compared to those described by Gantz, Weiss, Temares, and Sherron in Table 3.[64, 65, 66, 67] The terms are presented in a horizontal pattern to illustrate the similarity of the terms used in all five studies. The pattern also illustrates that even though Synnott and Gruber advocated the development of the Chief Information Officer concept, their role definitions are supported by later authors writing during the period of actual implementation.

Synnott, writing seven years after the publication of his treatise with Gruber and after serving as a Chief Information Officer, included his original descriptors in defining the functional CIO:

The CIO is responsible for the planning and architecture of the firm's information resources, for promoting information technology throughout the firm, and for looking after the corporation's investment in technology. The CIO manages information resources as a vital corporate asset . . . the CIOs are businessmen first, managers second, and technologists third . . . . The CIOs priorities, then, are: (1) concentrate on the business; (2) be a general manager; and (3) keep up with technology at the planning and managerial (not technical) level.[68]

In summary, the role and function of the Chief Information Officer evolved through a series of eras or stages that were influenced by the capabilities of information technology. The evolution of the technology from numerical data applications to the ability to provide and manipulate textual information created a decentralization of information management from a centralized source to departmental and individual use. The Chief Information Officer concept was established to facilitate the decentralization process and to manage a centralized infrastructure responsible for directing and maintaining that process.

Within that management role, the CIO has organization-wide responsibility based on the characteristics defined by Synnott and Gruber as listed in Table 3. The decentralization of information management and the organization-wide responsibilities of the CIO are indications of a transformation in the business sector. The next section discusses transformation and the role of information management.

Transformation Defined

Kilmann and Covin define transformation as an organization-wide application consequently referred to as "corporate transformation."

This is a process by which organizations examine what they were, what they are, what they will need to be, and how to make the necessary changes. Implementing those changes affects both psychological and strategic aspects of an organization. The term 'corporate' is used to convey the comprehensive effort required, in contrast to a piecemeal or single-division effort. 'Transformation' indicates the fundamental nature of change, in contrast to a mere linear extrapolation from the past. Corporate transformation is serious, large-scale change that demands new ways of perceiving, thinking, and behaving, by all members of the organization.[69]

Synnot & Gruber(1981)	Gantz (1985)	Weiss (1987)	Temares(1991)	Sherron(1988)
Strategic Planner	Strategic Planner	Partner in Planning	Strategic Planner	Planner
Change Agent		Innovator	Change Manager	Architect
Information Manager	Technological Literacy	Partner in applying applications	Partner in applying applications	Resource Manager
Proactivist		Innovator	Influencer	
Business Manager	General Business Manager	Partner in organization decision-making		
Politician	Negotiator	Negotiator		Communicator
Integrator		Innovator	Implementer	Architect
Information Controller			Implementer	
Staff Professional		Educator		Promoter
Manager	Decision-Maker at Staff Level	Awards Staff for Excellence		
Futurist			Visionary	

Table 3. CIO role and function.

Beckhard builds on Kilmann and Covin's definition by identifying four types of change that are transformational.[70] These are significant because Kilmann and Covin define transformation as "new ways of perceiving, thinking, and behaving by all members of the organization."[71] Beckhard's four types of transformational change provide a transition from definition to practice.

The types of changes that can be called transformational are:

1. Changes in what drives the organization—for example, a change from production driven or technology driven to market driven.
2. Fundamental changes in the relationship between the parts of the organization, that is, a redefinition of staff roles. This might mean moving from functionally driven to line-of-business driven, from centrally to decentrally managed, or from executive to strategic management.
3. Changes in the ways of doing work. Moving from low-technology to high-technology manufacturing systems; emphasizing the use of computers and telecommunications; and redesigning the customer interface by, for example, providing lap computers for salespeople so that they can interact directly with both customers and suppliers—these are transformational ways of doing things.
4. Basic cultural changes—that is, changes in norms, values, and rewards. For example, significantly rewarding people who produce an invention, whether it be a new business or changing to a system that rewards for flexibility, development, creativity of the organization, and rewards teamwork as well as individual effort.[72]

These types of changes all involve movement from a highly-structured to a more decentralized form of management. As pointed out earlier, information technology has caused a decentralization in the management of information. As will be shown, this is an example of the transformation to a decentralized organizational structure.

The highly structured approach to decision-making is the bureaucracy. The decentralized approach is the network or team concept. Morgan defines bureaucratic management as strictly adhering to a precise chain of command that rigidly follows prescribed rules and regulations. The administrative structure is clearly defined and employees in the organization are defined according to that structure and its rules and regulations. Bureaucracies "are places where individual initiative, enterprise, judgement, and creativity are supposed to take second place—if they are permitted at all!—to the politics and procedures that have been defined or authorized by those in charge of the organization . . ."[73]

Morgan identifies six organizational models arranged progressively from a strict bureaucracy to a completely open system. He contends that many organizations are in the process of transforming from model 1 to model 6.[74] Table 4 is an interpretation of the six models as they compare in terms of orientation, decision-making, communication, and organizational goal. In the movement from model 1 to model 6, hierarchical structure and control are increasingly deemphasized. The team approach to decision-making increases as hierarchical control decreases.

Morgan summarizes his comparison of the six models by stating that:

> A firm beginning as model 1 may over time evolve into models 2, 3, perhaps even 4. And if it is prepared to engage in a major "revolution," it may develop the features of models 5 and 6. But in reality, the transformation process from one end of the continuum to the other is extremely difficult to make, and the required change is more than structural—it is cultural and political as well.[75]

This statement is consistent with and supportive of Beckhard's contention, described earlier, that takes transformation from a bureaucracy/hierarchy to a more open organizational system. This involves a redesign of culture, politics, and goals.[76]

The Role of Information Management in the Transformation Process

Information management has become the facilitator of the transformation process. The sophistication of information technology and the resultant capabilities of managing information are creating an environment of decentralized management. This allows organizations to be more proactive in their approach to employing information management in the transformation process by providing groups and individuals with the capability to design and implement functions once under the exclusive domain of the information professional.[77, 78, 79, 80]

According to Hopper, the three following elements of decentralization will empower the transformation process:

[1] Powerful workstations will be a ubiquitous presence in offices and factories, and organizations will use them far more intensively and creatively than they do today . . . . [2] Companies will be technology architects rather than systems builders, even for their most critical applications. The widespread adoption of standards and protocols in hardware, software, and telecommunications will dramatically recast the technology management function . . . [3] Economies of scale will be more important than ever.[81]

This continued growth of decentralization, according to Hopper, creates a greater need for a centralized infrastructure because the amount of information needed to solve problems will grow exponentially. At the same

Model	Orientation	Decision-Making	Communication	Goal
1	Bureaucracy	Chief Executive Officer	Chain of command with every manager in an authoritarian role	Operate in an ultrastable (controlled) environment
2	Loose Bureaucracy	Management Team	From manager to subordinates with each manager having flexibility to be authoritarian or participative	Operate in a less controlled environment allowing some decentralization to head of principal departments
3	Hierarchically-controlled Network	Management Team	Project Teams that include lower level staff decisions are still made at the top of the organization	Operate in a structure that allows increased decentralization with lower lever staff having the ability to express opinions in the decision-making process
4	Matrix	Management Team with considerable influence from team leaders	Teams are formed ascending to function and product and include staff at all levels; team leaders are intrinsically involved in the decision-making process	Operate in a structure that gives product equal status with functional departmental organization giving employees more involvement in the decision-making process
5	Project Team Management	Team leaders in conjunction with senior management	Teams are dynamic, innovative, and equal to senior management in decision-making; communication is horizontal	Operate in an environment that causes an interaction of ideas and decisions among all employees; hierarchy is virtually meaningless
6	Loosely Coupled Network	Entire Staff	Horizontal among the staff, which is small and is responsible for planning and finances	Operate in an environment that allows all employees to set all goals and make all decisions together; the staff is small and all operations are contracted out

Table 4. Morgan's models of organizational orientation.

time, the capacity of telecommunications systems to transmit data will also grow exponentially. "The benefits of distributed computing will rely on access to vast amounts of data while collection, . . . storage, [and transmission] will be managed on a centralized basis."[82]

As indicated, a centralized infrastructure to manage information is even more important in an increasingly decentralized computing environment. The capabilities of information management allow organizations to be transformed through the provision of the information and communication systems necessary to plan, change, integrate, innovate, and manage in an environment with less control, that is, with less bureaucratic constraints.

> Most large companies are organized to reflect how information flows inside them. As electronic technologies create new possibilities for extending and sharing access to information, they make possible new kinds of organizations. Big companies will enjoy the benefits of scale without the burdens of bureaucracy. Information technology will drive the transition from corporate hierarchies to networks. Companies will become collections of experts who form teams to solve specific business problems and then disband. Information technology will blur distinctions between centralization and decentralization; senior managers will be able to contribute expertise without exercising authority . . . . Eventually, employees should be able to file their own insurance claims or check on their reimbursement status. With respect to bureaucratic procedures, the potential of an electronic platform is obvious: eliminate paper, slash layers, speed decisions, simplify the information flows.[83]

This ability of information management to not only facilitate but to drive the transformation process is supported by Nolan. He claims that information management allows the network structure to displace the traditional hierarchy. Information management allows a higher degree of sophistication of management and work by combining functions. Routine functions are being automated and are consequently disappearing. The result is fewer employees, reduced cost, and greater efficiency. Nolan further contends that if information management and the associated technology were removed, transformation would cease.[84]

Conclusion

The concepts of information management, chief information officer, and transformation are intertwined within the context of the successful employment of information technology. This chapter has provided an introduction to the concepts and the interrelationships involved. The chapters that follow expand upon these definitions and bring them into the reality of higher education and, by extension, the academic library.

Notes

1. *Oxford English Dictionary* (Oxford, England: Oxford University Press, 1989): 944.
2. Ibid., 945.
3. Donald A. Marchand, "Information Management: Strategies and Tools in Transition," *Information Management Review* 3: 27-34.
4. John F. Rockart, "The Line Takes the Leadership—IS Management in a Wired Society," *Sloan Management Review*, 29, no. 4: 57-64.
5. Jane N. Ryland, "Organizing and Managing Information Technology in Higher Education: A Historical Perspective," in *Organizing and Managing Information Resources on Campus*, ed. by Brian L. Hawkins (McKinney, TX: Academic Computing Publications, 1989): 17-32.
6. Marchand, 27-34.
7. Ryland, 17-32.
8. Rockart, 57-64.
9. Marchand, 27-34.
10. Ryland, 17-32.
11. Marchand, 27-34.
12. Judith A. Turner, "As Use of Computers Sweeps Campuses, Colleges Vie for Czars to Manage Them," *Chronicle of Higher Education* 28, no. 4: 1, 14.
13. Rockart, 57-64.
14. Marchand, 27-34.
15. Ibid., 32.
16. Ryland, 17-32.
17. Ibid., 17-32.
18. Kenneth C. Green, "A Perspective on Vendor Relationships: A Study of Symbiosis," in *Organizing and Managing Information Resources on Campus*, ed. by Brian L. Hawkins (McKinney, TX: Academic Computing Publications, 1989): 89-113.
19. Patricia Battin, "New Ways of Thinking about Financing Information Services" in *Organizing and Managing Information Resources on Campus*, ed. by Brian L. Hawkins (McKinney, TX: Academic Computing Publications, 1989): 369-383.
20. Ernest M. von Simson, "The Centrally Decentralized IS Organization," *Harvard Business Review* 68, no. 4: 158-162.
21. William R. Synnott, *The Information Weapon: Winning Customers and Markets with Technology* (New York: John Wiley & Sons, 1987).
22. Robert Robinson, "The Changing Agenda for Information Services: A Leadership Challenge," *CAUSE/EFFECT* 11, no. 3: 12-17.
23. Synnott, 23.
24. Robinson, 12-17.
25. J. Gary Auguston, "Strategies for Financial Planning," in *Organizing and Managing Information Resources on Campus*, ed. by Brian L. Hawkins (McKinney, TX: Academic Computing Publications, 1989): 263-279.

26. Ryland, 17-32.
27. James I. Penrod and Michael G. Dolence, "Managing Information Technology: Facing the Issues," *Proceedings of the 1989 CAUSE National Conference* (Boulder, CO: CAUSE, 1990): 71-81.
28. Anne Woodsworth, *Patterns and Options for Managing Information Technology on Campus* (Chicago, American Library Association: 1991).
29. Green, 89-113.
30. Russell S. Vaught, "Organizing and Supporting Administrative Computing," in *Organizing and Managing Information Resources on Campus*, ed. by Brian L. Hawkins (McKinney, TX: Academic Computing Publications, 1989):141-163.
31. Ibid., 141-163.
32. Brian L. Hawkins, "Preparing for the Next Wave of Computing on Campus," *Change* 23, no. 1: 24-31.
33. Brian L. Hawkins, Ronald F. E. Weissman, and Don C. Wolfe, "Prescriptions for Managing Information Resources on Campus," in *Organizing and Managing Information Resources on Campus*, ed. by Brian L. Hawkins (McKinney, TX: Academic Computing Publications, 1989): 229-259.
34. Ibid., 229-259.
35. Vaught, 141-163.
36. Brian L. Hawkins, "Introduction: Managing a Revolution— Turning a Paradox into a Paradigm," in *Organizing and Managing Information Resources on Campus,* ed. by Brian L. Hawkins (McKinney, TX: Academic Computing Publications, 1989): 1-14.
37. James I. Penrod, "Creating CIO Positions," *Proceedings of the 1985 CAUSE National Conference* (Boulder, CO: CAUSE, 1986): 40-41.
38. Ibid.
39. Woodsworth.
40. James C. Emery, "Issues in Building an Information Technology Strategy," *EDUCOM Bulletin* 19, no. 3: 4-13.
41. James I. Penrod, Michael G. Dolence, and Judith V. Douglas, *The Chief Information Officer in Higher Education* (Boulder, CO: CAUSE, 1990).
42. Ibid.
43. Woodsworth.
44. Penrod, Dolence, and Douglas, *The Chief Information Officer in Higher Education.*
45. Hawkins, "Preparing for the Next Wave of Computing on Campus," 24-31.
46. Battin, 369-370.
47. Synnott, 22.
48. Ryland, 17-32.
49. James I. Penrod and Michael G. Dolence, "IRM a Short Lived Concept?," *Proceedings of the 1987 CAUSE National Conference* (Boulder, CO: CAUSE, 1988): 173-183.
50. Rockart, 57-64.
51. Penrod and Dolence, "IRM a Short Lived Concept?," 173-183.
52. Rockart, 57-64.
53. Ibid., 57-64.
54. Ibid., 63.
55. Synnott, 19.
56. John Gantz, "Telecommunications Management: Who's in Charge?," *Telecommunication Products + Technology* (October, 1985): 17-37.
57. Turner, 1, 14.

58. Auguston, 268.
59. Harry L. Dillman and Morris A. Hicks, "Reorganizing for Information Technology Management on Campus," *CAUSE/EFFECT* 13, no. 3: 4-6.
60. Penrod, Dolence, and Douglas, *The Chief Information Officer in Higher Education.*
61. Woodsworth, 9.
62. William R. Synnott and William H. Gruber, *Information Resource Management: Opportunities and Strategies for the 1980s* (New York: John Wiley & Sons, 1981).
63. Ibid.
64. Gantz, 17-37.
65. Madeline Weiss, "Transformers," *CIO Magazine* (September/October, 1987): 37-41.
66. M. Lewis Temares, "Future Directions in Higher Education: A CIO's Perspective," *Proceedings of the 1990 CAUSE National Conference* (Boulder, CO: CAUSE, 1991): 47-57.
67. Gene T. Sherron, "Organizing to Manage Information Resources," *Proceedings of the 1987 CAUSE National Conference* (Boulder, CO: CAUSE, 1988): 185-195.
68. Synnott, 19, 23, 25.
69. Ralph H. Kilmann and Teresa Joyce Covin, "Preface," in *Corporate Transformation: Revitalizing Organizations for a Competitive World,* ed. by Ralph H. Kilmann and Teresa Joyce Covin (San Francisco: Jossey Bass, 1988): xiii-xviii.
70. Richard Beckhard, "The Executive Management of Transformational Change," in *Corporate Transformation: Revitalizing Organizations for a Competitive World,* ed. by Ralph H. Kilmann and Teresa Joyce Covin (San Francisco: Jossey Bass, 1988): 89-101.
71. Kilmann and Covin, xix.
72. Beckhard, 91.
73. Garth Morgan, *Creative Organization Theory: A Resourcebook* (Newbury Park, CA: Sage, 1989).
74. Ibid.
75. Ibid.
76. Beckhard, 89-101.
77. Max D. Hopper, "Rattling SABRE—New Ways to Compete on Information," *Harvard Business Review* 68, no. 3: 118-124.
78. DuWayne J. Peterson, "Letter to the Editor," *Harvard Business Review* 11, no. 3: 180-181.
79. Richard L. Nolan, "Too Many Executives Today Just Don't Get It!," *CAUSE/EFFECT* 13, no. 4: 5-11.
80. James I. Penrod and Michael G. Dolence, "Concepts for Reengineering in Higher Education," *CAUSE/EFFECT* 14, no. 2: 10-17.
81. Hopper, 119-120.
82. Ibid., 120
83. Ibid., 125.
84. Nolan, 5-11.

Information Management and the Transformation of Higher Education

Jane Norman Ryland

Introduction

Transformation is a "hot" topic on many college and university campuses today. But how many institutions make the connection that information technology might have a role in transformation initiatives underway? College and university presidents are immersed in concerns, as is only appropriate, about the harsh realities of a bleak economic climate, about competing for the best faculty, students, and staff, and about improving the quality of education and research. Information technology, if viewed as a means to help institutions accomplish their missions in a new and better way rather than an end in itself, may provide some answers.

Despite computers having been around for some time, it is only now that several elements have matured simultaneously to open the untapped potential of technology applied to the management of information: the possibility of a ubiquitous network removing barriers of time and place, sufficient speed to make viable multimedia information resources allowing emulation of a full range of sensory interactions, new models for scholarly publication and scholarly communication offering the promise of navigation in the ever-increasing flood of information, and the ability to involve students in a comingled interactive process of teaching and learning.

In a transformed institution, faculty, students, administrators, and executives all find it easier to do business, achieve higher levels of quality, and maintain cost-effectiveness. For the first time, statistics are showing not just qualitative gains but real dollar savings as well through the use of information technology.

Transformation—A "Hot" Topic

An article in the September 12, 1990, issue of *The Chronicle of Higher Education* may have been the first clue that transformation was becoming a "hot"

22

topic on college and university campuses. The front page story reported prominent university presidents at Cornell, Stanford, the University of Michigan, Indiana, Northwestern, Iowa State, and elsewhere proclaiming the advent of change "as fundamental as the great transformations that swept higher education more than a century ago . . ."[1] These leaders are calling for changes in virtually every aspect of higher education, including the creation of more effective methods for teaching and learning, establishment of new criteria for promoting and granting tenure to faculty, and reform of such basic operational practices as management and funding.

While improving quality, especially of the teaching and learning process, was often mentioned as one of the goals of the transformation initiatives, a closer look suggests that the financial motivation is paramount, with "transformation" viewed as one way to react positively to the economic pressures increasingly burdening higher education. Years of tuition increases that outstrip the increases in the consumer price index, research overhead expense (and particularly the administrative component) coming under increased scrutiny, and growing public dissatisfaction with higher education outcomes combine to create the expectation of fewer dollars available but no diminution of demand for an educated citizenry to meet the challenges of the highly competitive globalized society of the future.

The transformation movement is apparently not limited to major research universities; at a meeting of the League for Innovation in the Community College in 1991, a show of hands in a general session indicated that many community colleges have transformation initiatives underway as well.

In the business world, the concept of transformation is even more familiar but not necessarily any better understood than it is in higher education. In his keynote address at the 1989 CAUSE National Conference in San Diego, California, Richard Nolan asserted that executives in the business world, while universally having heard the term "transformation," "just don't get it," don't understand what transformation is and what must be done to transform their organizations.[2]

Nolan contends that transformation entails a change in how any organization operates to match the new rules of the Information Economy which is rapidly supplanting the Industrial Economy of the past forty or fifty years. He goes on to enumerate the elements of the transformation he believes to be essential. At the heart of Nolan's definition of a transformed organization is replacement of the functional hierarchy by a flexible network structure, with fewer individuals playing roles dedicated to operational and clerical tasks and more functioning as knowledge workers enabled by technology and access to electronic information resources.

While Nolan has focused his attention primarily on the corporate world rather than higher education, he includes colleges and universities within the realm of entities that must transform in order to succeed in the future. Information technology professionals in colleges and universities who were asked to react to Nolan's arguments by and large agreed with him, but differed on how higher education might achieve transformation and how likely this would be to happen.[3]

Not surprisingly, information technology/information management organizations and officers are viewed as a key element in the transformation all believe needs to happen. Information technology leaders, after all, are in a position to recognize the contributions technology might make. For some time, in order to successfully achieve their objectives, information technology organizations have had to marshal support and collaboration from individuals in diverse segments of the campus community. Development of automated systems for campus users has encouraged the formation of such groups and created a need for the kind of networked organization Nolan describes, where the project managers do not have line responsibility for the rest of the group/ team members. As the information technology professionals noted in their responses to Nolan's article, too often a CEO delegates the task of transformation through technology to his or her information technology leader, without realizing that transformation initiatives require strong leadership and personal participation from chief executives.

Reactions of college and university presidents to Nolan's challenges, compiled in a subsequent issue of *CAUSE/EFFECT*, echo many of the beliefs of the information technology professionals, especially in looking to those IT leaders to play a critical role in educating and "transforming" the presidents.[4] While for the most part agreeing with Nolan, they fault him for applying a predominantly manufacturing model to higher education, and most believe that transformation is already happening, at least on *their* campuses.

A related concept is "re-engineering," a concept described by Penrod and Dolence as a process of "reexamining basic assumptions about the way we do things . . . , redesigning work processes based upon new assumptions; . . . refusing to be limited by traditions of the past."[5] This term has been slower to gain recognition. In a November 1991 CAUSE Postcard Survey, only 18 percent of CAUSE campus representatives responding ranked re-engineering among their top three priorities. When responses are analyzed by Carnegie classification, research universities as a group indicated the most interest, with 30 percent identifying it as a priority. However, re-engineering appears to be gaining momentum: at the 1991 CAUSE National Conference a month later, the concept was frequently mentioned in formal and informal discussions.

But how do these institutions make the connection that information technology and information management might play a role in their transformation initiatives? In the September 1990 *Chronicle* article, only one university president made even the briefest mention of technology as a part of broader transformation goals; James J. Duderstadt, president of the University of Michigan, identified as one of his three goals the meeting of challenges presented by the approaching "'Age of Knowledge,' especially through the introduction of state-of-the-art computer networks and systems."[6]

Typically, college and university presidents and chancellors are focused on finding sufficient financial resources to operate and update existing sytems. Many are aware of the constraints of space, with deteriorating physical facilities, for which insufficient monies have been set aside as deferred maintenance, and insufficient shelf space in libraries to store even a decreasing percentage of the burgeoning volume of new knowledge being published in printed form—assuming funds are available to keep up with the skyrocketing cost of serials. For the first time, concepts of competition and strategic advantage are being discussed in college board rooms, not just to attract and retain students but to replace retiring faculty from a dwindling supply of recent graduates of doctoral studies.

For those of us who work with information technology and information management, it is easy see the possibilities for information technology to facilitate transformation. However, for those outside the information technology profession, especially for those in chief executive positions, information technology may instead look more like a black hole into which untold resources, both financial and human, may be absorbed with little to show for the investment—just one more special interest competing for the shrunken resource pool. Information technology and information management, if viewed as a means to help institutions accomplish their missions in a new and better way, rather than as an end in itself, may provide some answers to all of these challenges and also be a means for enabling transformation to occur. In viewing technology as an means rather than an end, however, it is important, as Jim Penrod contends, that it be viewed not just as a tool for doing the same thing that has always been done.[7] This might be a necessary first step, but technology's real power is as a tool for accomplishing something in an entirely new way, a "transformed" way.

How can information technology and information management be harnessed positively to help achieve the transformation we desperately want and need?

A Confluence of Capabilities

Firstly, the proliferation of powerful desktop computers in the 1980s has given way to initiatives for connectivity, with local area networks connecting departmental systems, high-speed backbones making the connections across the campus, and state and regional networks providing links to other institutions across the country and around the world via the Internet and BITNET. More than just connecting computer to computer, these networks link people to each other and to information resources. Information management, accomplished through the facilitating powers of technology, makes it possible to put the right information in the hands of the people who need it, at the right time. By removing the barriers of time and place, the network will play a key role in making the transformation of higher education a reality.

Passage of legislation in late 1991 to create a National Research and Education Network (NREN) will hasten the availability of a ubiquitous high-speed network to all of higher education and even to many allied commercial entities. Plans for the NREN are to build on networks already in place rather than create a new one. The National Science Foundation Network (NSFNET), that already links supercomputer resources across the United States and ties in many colleges and universities through regional networks, has been termed the Interim Interagency NREN, or IINREN, and will be augmented to gigabit transmission capabilities to become the NREN of the future.

Secondly, computer speeds have always been viewed as incredibly fast and storage capacities incredibly vast; in fact, they have been barely sufficient. For a long time, computers processed numbers, and then numbers and words together. Only recently have increases in speed and storage capacity opened the possibility of adding images and sound. Eventually, we will have the ability to emulate a wide range of sensory interaction with technology, adding motion, color, three dimensions, and speech input/output or handwriting instead of keyboarding. The information we will be able to manage through these new technologies will be quite different from the numerical and textual information we associate with today's computers and technology.

This will have two major implications for the transformation of higher education: the ability to automatically change from one form to another, as when a musical score is converted to a musical performance; and the ability to simulate interaction with the past or future, as when a student can carry on a simulated dialog with Einstein or predict the results of global warming twenty years hence.

Third, information management and information technology will make it possible to transform the processes of scholarly communication and publication, functions that are at the heart of the higher education enterprise. Scholars have begun to describe how new models of scholarly communication will work.[8] The Coalition for Networked Information (CNI), a project of the Association of Research Libraries, CAUSE, and EDUCOM, was begun in 1990 to bring together the stakeholders in current processes of scholarly communication and publication to identify and resolve the problems that stand in the way of ensuring the widespread availability of electronic information resources via networks. As the virtual library becomes a reality, higher education itself will be transformed.

Fourth, we are beginning to recognize the value of applying technology to involve students in the learning process. The old Chinese proverb, "I hear and I forget; I see and I remember; I do and I understand," holds true; involvement is the key to real learning. Watching a demonstration of IBM's "Ulysses," a multimedia package for teaching Tennyson's poem, instantly conveys the power of technology to involve the student and light the fire of excitement that learning *can* bring but too seldom does.

A Transformation Scenario

How can these elements work together to bring about a transformation in higher education? The following scenario assumes no more technological capability than exists somewhere, in some form, today, but rarely are all capabilities found on a single campus.

A prospective student's first casual contact with the transformed college receives an immediate, personalized follow-up from the admissions office, where transcripts from high school and any other college coursework taken anywhere are collected and transmitted electronically via networks. An electronic profile match indicates a high probability for success. With the prospective student having been identified as highly desirable, the college's personalized response might contain statistics from a nation-wide networked database reflecting outcomes for previous students with similar backgrounds after completing college. A scan of the college's own database quickly identifies alumni in the prospective student's neighborhood who are called upon to help "market" the college (it's clear the alumni were happy with their college experience by the record of their annual donations!).

The fast, personalized response of the transformed college pays off: the prospective student decides to enroll. Like many students today, this one holds a full-time job and has child care responsibilities, making it difficult to travel the twenty miles from home to campus. In the transformed college, this is no longer a problem. Information about courses offered, faculty, and schedules is available through the electronic campus-wide information system, as is information on special events, jobs available, and how to register for classes. It's a pleasant surprise to the student that even registration can be accomplished without standing in long lines in the gymnasium; any touch-tone phone is all that is needed. Classes are offered not only on the main campus but also in remote conference facilities, one in the student's own neighborhood, where the two-way interactive video link enables direct involvement in the classroom discussion and not just passive listening to a lecture.

Course materials were custom-selected by the professor, compiled from numerous works with only the relevant chapters included, and printed on demand on campus. Some of the course materials are references to electronic publications available on the network; their electronic form is not just a convenience to facilitate searching for specific references, but in some cases a necessity, since the printed page cannot possibly accommodate such new forms as three-dimensional color motion visualizations of scientific experiments.

Homework assignments are found by logging on to the network. Questions about the assignments are easily clarified by an e-mailed question to the professor, and many of the assignments involve collaborative work with classmates, where, once again, barriers of time and place are eliminated by the network. Several of the longer-term group assignments offer the time to participate in electronic discussion groups with students at other institutions, and even in other countries, or with relevant work experience, whose diverse perspectives bring new levels of understanding. Access to library resources, once difficult to arrange when a trip to the library meant coordinating library hours, class schedules, work schedules, transportation, and parking, is available twenty-four hours a day, seven days a week, because the transformed library has no walls and is as close as the nearest terminal or workstation. And at the end of the semester the student can check his or her grades—and, scholarship and student loan status—via modem or touch-tone phone without leaving home.

For the faculty member in the transformed college, it is rewarding to be able to reach more students without spending more time, yet enhance interaction with students and provide more personal attention. Professors who participate in teaching via interactive two-way video links report that interaction with students in a remote location, when the video camera can zoom in for a close-up of the student's face, can "feel" more personally interactive than trying to pick out the face of a questioning student from the sea of faces in a lecture room of three hundred.

Advising students, once a chore made difficult by finding time in busy schedules for personal meetings, is facilitated in the transformed college when personal meetings can be supplemented with electronic communications, and student profiles are readily available electronically to the advisors.

Communication with colleagues around the world enhances the work experience of faculty; the availability of such communication electronically is commonplace in the transformed college, with active discussion groups on a broad range of topics and the ability to share experimental results and research. Electronic dissemination of preliminary efforts can quickly invoke peer review, and electronic journals can carry authenticated work to other researchers and directly to industry for practical application. The professor in the transformed college can describe for the network a profile of specific interests, and as new material is published electronically, all material matching the profile is automatically flagged for later perusal, storage, or printing.

The presidents and chancellors in the transformed college are delighted with the summary information available at their fingertips. Having identified critical success factors for the operation of the institution, they are able to choose color graphic displays of enrollments by program, revenues, costs, and facilities utilization, showing current status in comparison to historical statistics for the institution. Comparative information for similar institutions nationally is readily available on the network from national professional associations. Models help to predict future demand and identify potential problems; investment and cash flow analysis is facilitated. With such timely and accurate information, the president can confidently decide to capitalize on a newly presented opportunity or to pursue a joint venture with a local manufacturer.

We've already seen how the functions of the admissions office and registrar are made more efficient and effective in the transformed college. Administrators in every other area find advantages as well. For the purchasing department, network linkages to suppliers make it easy to check on availability, specifications, and competitive pricing. Orders placed electronically save time and money, with funds transferred electronically to the vendor's account at just the right time to maximize discounts available versus retention of funds in interest-bearing accounts. In the alumni/development office, fundraising appeals are automatically personalized and targeted; donations are up in the transformed college.

A striking observation in the transformed college is the apparent level of satisfaction and well being. Faculty, students, administrators, and executives all find it easier to do business, achieve higher levels of quality, and maintain cost-effectiveness.

For students, it's easy to obtain needed information, register for and attend classes, and gain access to faculty. The process of learning is less difficult and more interesting, and there is satisfaction in knowing not only that they are receiving solid preparation for good jobs in the real world, but that the skills gained in dealing with electronic information resources will carry over to their future lives.

For faculty, electronic information resources via the network help make teaching, research, and communication with colleagues more effective. Student interaction is enhanced and information technology allows more effective use of time by facilitating routine administrative tasks.

For administrators, it's easier to accomplish normal duties and offer the personalized service that yields results. Timely information is readily available to enhance decision-making.

Presidents, chancellors, and trustees are delighted to find that their transformed college is in high demand. Students, faculty, and administrators want to be a part of the campus community. Perhaps equally satisfying is the cost containment benefit. More students are being served with the same level of resources, but quality and interaction are enhanced. It's true that a larger percentage of resources are now devoted to information technology, especially to training and deferred maintenance to ensure that systems are kept up to date, but the most costly resources—faculty and facilities—are being used more cost-effectively, and administrators are supporting a larger operation through greater levels of productivity.

A Groundswell of Evidence

Historically, information technologists in higher education have done little in the way of cost justification for the investment in technology and information management. Early claims that automation would result in reduced personnel invariably were disproved. Within the last few years, however, concrete evidence of cost savings as well as qualitative improvements is emerging.

The National Association of College and University Business Officers (NACUBO), with sponsorship from the USX Foundation, Inc., presents annual cost reduction incentive awards recognizing innovative cost-saving ideas implemented by colleges and universities. A similar program is sponsored by the Canadian Association of University Business Officers with support from the The Royal Bank of Canada, The Molson Companies, and the Power Corporation of Canada. Monetary awards in both programs range from $100 to $10,000, and proposals for the awards record millions of dollars in savings each year.

For the last two years, information management systems have dominated awards in NACUBO's program, with the 1990 winner, Pennsylvania State University, documenting $740,000 in savings with a system for electronic generation, approval, and storage of business forms across a campus-wide network.[9] Other award winners have included a system for the online preparation of internal budgets, an automated loans receivable coupon system, a paperless process to document cost transfers, a paperless loan application system, a bar-coded parking system, a service to provide student financial data by touch-tone telephone, automated calculation of pension contributions, computerized time accounting, consolidation of telecommunications functions, and countless other instances where technology and information management are saving real dollars.

On the qualitative side, an article in the January/February 1991 issue of *Change* magazine recorded striking improvements in several areas, but especially in the examination scores of students associated with the introduction of electronic tutorials in English composition classes.[10]

In late 1989, Chancellor Joe B. Wyatt of Vanderbilt University challenged the attendees at the 1989 EDUCOM national conference to "identify one hundred success stories where information technologies had made a difference in undergraduate education."[11] Stories selected from the hundreds nominated document conclusively that technology, applied to the tasks of information management, is making a real difference, both quantitatively and qualitatively, in the classroom, in the dissemination of campus-wide information, in student record-keeping, in education for the disabled student, in the submission and grading of assignments, and for collaborative student interaction.

An article in the summer 1991 issue of *College & University*, the quarterly journal of the American Association of Collegiate Registrars and Admissions Officers, provided the first conclusive evidence of cost effectiveness of touch-tone telephone registration systems, first implemented in the United States at Brigham Young University in 1986 and adopted in concept by nearly 200 institutions since.[12] In addition to overwhelmingly positive responses of touch-tone registration users, significant savings are accrued in the improved use of faculty and classroom facility space, two of the most costly resources for any institution. Tables 1 and 2 show, for pre- and post-touch-tone registration time periods at Brigham Young, significant decreases in the total classroom seats made available and, more dramatically, in the unused seats at the close of the enrollment period and in the difference between the number of seats occupied at beginning enrollment and at final enrollment.

While these studies and reports are encouraging, others have shown disappointing results from technology investments, with no reported improvement financially or qualitatively. What accounts for these disparities? Perhaps too often we easily recognize the potential of technology and information management to achieve transformation and then expect it to just happen, ignoring the long and difficult processes of making change happen, especially changing people and changing behavior.

Barriers to Transformation

Barriers persist on the pathway to achieving the vision of an institution transformed through information management. Identification of the barriers, however, is the first step in an action plan to help overcome them and achieve transformation.

The first barrier is the need for still more investment in technological infrastructure, training, and maintenance. Especially in these times of economic hardship, it is difficult to justify spending money on technology. Considerable investments have already been made, accompanied by promises of results which have not always been achieved. With technological change occurring so rapidly, the mainframes and minicomputers purchased only a few years ago have little residual value, and performance characteristics that may not even match today's powerful workstations. When forced into choices between terminating faculty and staff or adding hardware, it is often impossible to make purely objective decisions.

Just because a network exists doesn't mean that everyone will immediately have access to it, and thus, to their colleagues and the world's knowledge store. We are still years away from every faculty member, administrator, executive, and student having a microcomputer, workstation, or even a terminal for individual use, and sharing such resources dramatically reduces the likelihood of use. Despite the exponential growth in numbers of institutions attaching to the Internet and in network traffic, many institutions are not yet connected, and "have" and "have not" departments exist even on the leading-edge resource-rich campuses. An article in the December 4, 1991, issue of *The Chronicle of Higher Education* pointed out that despite the investment committed by Congressional legislation in the NREN, the bulk of the investment must come from the campus level, and small institutions in particular may find themselves denied access.[13]

Pre- and Post-Touch-Tone Registration Periods

	Fall '83	% of Total	Fall '89	% of Total	# Diff.	% Change
Total seats made available	206,597	100	187,408	100	-19,189	-9.3
Seats occupied at close of enrollment period	144,221	69.8	144,706	77.2	+485	0.03
Unused seats at close of enrollment period	62,376	30.2	42,702	22.9	-19,674	-31.5

Note: These data are based on daytime enrollment for Fall 1983 of 26,963 and Fall 1989 of 27,112 or +.6 percent.

Table 1. Source: Adapted from material in Robert W. Spencer, "'After' the Registration Revolution." College & University, Summer 1991, 211. Reprinted with permission from American Association of Collegiate Registrars and Admissions Officers.

Table 2.

	Beginning Enrollment (seats occupied)	Final Enrollment	# Diff.	% Change
Fall 1983	126,098	144,221	+18,123	+14.4
Fall 1989	136,392	144,706	+9,314	+6.0
Difference	+10,294	+485	8,809	
Percent	8.2	0.003	48.6	

Note: These data are based on daytime enrollment for Fall 1983 of 26,963 and Fall 1989 of 27,112 or +.6 percent.

Table 2. Adapted from material in Robert W. Spencer, "'After' the Registration Revolution." College & University, Summer 1991, 211. Reprinted with permission from American Association of Collegiate Registrars and Admissions Officers.

Ease of use of technology has improved considerably with the popularity of graphic user interfaces, but here too there is much more to be accomplished. Using technology should be as easy as using a television. Even the most omnipresent of software, word processing, is rarely used to its full potential; unless features are used regularly they are overlooked when the need for them does present itself. Ease of use has different meanings for the regular user and the infrequent user; both levels must be satisfied. A related barrier is insufficient training. Too often, resources and capabilities go unused because the investment in technology was not followed by the equally essential investment in training. An unexpected barrier to achieving transformation through information management comes from using technology inappropriately. Enforced or inappropriate use of technology, when doing something "the old way" would have been much better, produces far more harm than benefit.

Many of the electronic newsletters introduced in recent months are simply conversions from their printed forms. These are often ill-suited to electronic presentation, with the reader having no option but to scroll through screen after screen, unable to go directly to the one or two articles of interest.

Inefficient printing out and filing of the newsletter often negate all the advantages of the electronic publication. Some unmoderated electronic discussion groups also fall prey to misuse, with subscription messages and notices of absences going by mistake to hundreds of list subscribers.

We sometimes erroneously assume that the new technology must replace the old rather than offering a new technique to be used when appropriate. Electronic mail capability does not eliminate the value of making a phone call or writing a letter; the capability to access journals and other information resources electronically does not suggest that no more books and journals need be printed.

Transformation may not be achievable as quickly and easily as many of us may wish. A gradual evolution may be inevitable rather than revolutionary change; trying to achieve change too quickly can create obstacles. A first step might be simple improvement or modernization, replacing an old approach with a new one. Once use of new technologies is begun, the seeds are sown for the second step of innovation to occur. Innovation can then lead to transformation. Quantum leaps are less likely to occur. When the printing press first made possible the rapid replication and dissemination of knowledge, the first printed products mimicked the familiar illuminated manuscripts which had been created individually by hand.

Perhaps a first step in the transformation to electronic scholarly communication and publication will be to retain the form of the printed publication for the reader but reverse the timing of the print and distribution processes. Electronic distribution followed by printing on demand, retaining full integrity of the author's and publisher's intent for printed form, could replace the current system of printing followed by distribution of the printed documents.

New concepts and new technologies also often require a "gestation" period of subconscious thought before being understood and accepted. An initiative called the Alexandria Institute in the early 1980s had goals strikingly similar to those of the Coalition for Networked Information; CNI has captured a level of interest and support from the higher education, library, publishing, and information technology communities never attained by the Alexandria Institute.

Perhaps the most difficult barrier is that transformation necessitates transforming people and how they act. Making available a new technological capability doesn't guarantee that it will be used. The time cycle for changing personal behavior is much longer than the time cycle for technological advance. Too often we make the mistake of ignoring the "people" factor in the transformation equation.

An Action Plan for Transformation

A plan to achieve the vision of transformation starts with securing commitment and advocacy from the top. There is a small but growing number of institutional presidents and chancellors who are enthusiastic advocates for the application of technology to transform higher education. More frequently, the chief executive is preoccupied with other challenges; in the worst case, technology (and the technology advocate) is a pariah.

To gain the ear of the president, the technology advocate must speak the language of the president, not just eliminating jargon, acronyms, and technological arrogance, but viewing situations from the perspective of the whole institution. The president is unlikely to respond to a recitation of the features of the latest workstation, software, or local area network, but may respond to a presentation or discussion about how the institution can reach new constituencies through distance education, improve the quality of classroom instruction, enhance the productivity of administrators, or facilitate better decision-making through access to information resources.

Once commitment from the top is in place, transformation initiatives can begin to spread to others on campus. It may take hard work, one-on-one, to inspire others with the same vision, but it can happen, especially if the advocate is first willing to enroll in the vision of the individual. Spending time with deans, professors, and administrators, and doing more listening than talking, can foster the necessary understanding and the basis for the first steps to transformation.

Those on campus who are most susceptible are usually easily identified; they can be "enlisted" to help "recruit" their colleagues. Actual demonstrations can drive home the benefits of transformation through technology much more quickly than simple conversation; videotapes currently available, showing ordinary people using off-the-shelf hardware, can—in the absence of actual demonstrations—also be effective in inspiring others.

The passion that drives the technology advocate should not be a passion to deliver technology to students, faculty, executives, and administrators, but a passion to deliver quality services to our shared clientele and to develop educated, productive citizens and members of the future workforce of our country and the world. Most of us would accept a special assignment from our presidents to take on an additional five hours a week beyond current workloads to make a significant contribution to our institutions. Why shouldn't we take the initiative independently to understand institutional goals and seek out ways for information technology to help achieve those goals?

Strategic planning is an important element in achieving a vision of transformation. Planning for the application of information technologies and information management cannot be done in isolation; technology planning must be part of an institution's overall strategic planning process. Whether formal or informal, resulting in a written plan or in informal consensus, it is likely that some type of strategic planning exists on every campus.

A strategic plan for technology should include clear goals and objectives, formulated with broad participation from the entire campus community. Where possible, tangible, visible indicators of success should be identified. These might include objectives for placement of graduates, external recognition of faculty, or evidence of student preparation to enter the workforce rather than the incorporation of technology use into a certain percentage of classes. The right incentives can be effective in helping achieve transformation through information management. For faculty, the traditional motivating forces of promotion and tenure can play a role, but not just for using technology in the classroom, developing instructional courseware, or publishing in an electronic journal. The focus should be on contributions to enhancing the quality of education, advancing research and scholarship, or improving productivity through the use of technology.

For students, the entertainment factor may provide the initial incentive. Entertainment, in the sense of holding attention agreeably, not the sense of passing time uselessly, can "seduce" the student into learning and instill the excitement of learning that can subsequently be satisfied by more traditional and less entertaining forms of learning.

For administrators as well as faculty and students, the incentive can come in the form of the seductive application which obviously achieves the desired result with less effort and time. If the access point to technology—the microcomputer or workstation—is in the next room instead of on one's desk, it is much less likely to be used. If teaching, learning, communication with colleagues, communication with students, and access to needed information are easier with technology, then the technological solution will be chosen.

The ability to enhance quality through the technological solution may be an incentive, but it is human nature to weigh the cost versus expected benefit. When the benefit of enhanced quality comes at the price of too much time, effort, and money, it's not worth it.

To help achieve transformation through information management, sufficient training and assistance must be made available. It may not be possible for an institution to provide enough dedicated human resources to satisfy the need for training and support. Many institutions are exploring alternatives such as directories of faculty, administrators, and students with expertise in specific technologies who are willing to be called on for assistance.

Transformation ultimately requires a rethinking of the desired result. Is the desired result of education to transfer a body of knowledge on a specific subject, for a profession, or in a discipline? Or is it to convey the ability to determine what needs to be learned, how to locate the necessary information, how to assess and evaluate information to make decisions, how to work collaboratively to glean ideas from interaction, and how to solve problems and complete projects? Or is it to instill the skills needed to be a productive worker and contributing member of society?

It is important for an action plan to allow sufficient time for transformation. It may not be possible to move directly to transformation; improvement or modernization efforts may have to come first, laying the groundwork for innovation to flourish. It is likely that the most significant transformations that information technology may make possible ten years from now are entirely unanticipated today.

The simple transfer, for example, of a passive approach of teaching by lecture to teaching via a television monitor, does not constitute transformation. Where computer conferencing and discussion groups have been used to facilitate collaborative work on research and homework assignments; where access to the library's information resources is not bounded by the library's open hours, having to get to the library physically, or by a single library's collection; where written results are shared electronically, soliciting diverse perspectives including those of practicing professionals in the field, results can be achieved similar to the small seminars all but the most exclusive institutions have been forced to move away from. It is essential to rethink the outcome desired and work backward with the tools of information technology in mind.

Finally, it is important to take advantage of opportunities to share ideas that work and learn from the experiences of others. Conferences and publications will have a significant role in the spread of transformation on college and university campuses and, ultimately, into the infrastructure of our society.

Summary

The key to transformation through information technology and information management lies in weaving technology into the very fabric of the institution, so thoroughly that the capabilities of technology are well understood, readily available, and automatically considered as one of the tools available to meet the challenges, solve the problems, and accomplish the objectives of the institution.

Reviewing institutional strategic plans can be an insightful exercise. Consistently, missions, goals, and objectives suggest countless opportunities where information technology can make a difference, yet rarely are technology solutions identified.

A typical institutional mission today might include the objective of improving the quality of education. Technology can involve and engage the student in an active learning process, improve student support services including registration and access to campus-wide information, and achieve true excellence in teaching and advisement.

Another institutional objective commonly identified is to develop and strengthen research. In every institution—not just major research universities but liberal arts, comprehensive, and community colleges as well—there is continual ongoing research by faculty keeping current in their disciplines, and by students in their normal work assignments. Technology is transforming the entire process of scholarly communication and scholarly publication via the network, making possible easy and widespread contact with colleagues and access to the world's ever-expanding store of recorded knowledge, even as it is being developed.

Another institutional objective frequently encountered might be providing access to education for under-represented groups. For ethnic minorities with language difficulties, technology can ease the transition to English with native language interfaces. Institutions with large populations of students for whom English is a second language are offering such services as front ends for registration systems in a wide range of languages, including Chinese. Technology can facilitate the participation of students in rural areas via distance education; these services can also reach parents with children at home and full-time workers who can't otherwise travel to campus to attend classes during the day.

An institutional objective of contributing to the economy of the community can be achieved by producing a trained workforce familiar with technology as a tool for accessing information and for collaborative work, the norm for the leading businesses of today and the expected transformed businesses of tomorrow—and hopefully also for the transformed institutions of higher education in the not too distant future.

Notes

1. Karen Grassmuck, "Some Research Universities Contemplate Sweeping Changes, Ranging From Management and Tenure to Teaching Methods," *The Chronicle of Higher Education* (12 September 1990): A1, A29-A31.
2. Richard L. Nolan, "Too Many Executives Today Just Don't Get It!" *CAUSE/EFFECT* (Winter 1990): 5-11.
3. David L. Smallen, Carole Barone, Dorothy Hopkin, James I. Penrod, and Kenneth Blythe. "What Will It Take to 'Get It' in Higher Education?" *CAUSE/EFFECT* (Winter 1990): 11-15.
4. Richard D. Breslin, David M. Clarke, Joseph Cronin, Thomas Ehrlich, Donald N. Langenberg, Harold McAninch, and Donald C. Swain. "Transforming Higher Education in the Information Age: Presidents Respond." *CAUSE/EFFECT* (Fall 1991): 6-12.
5. James I. Penrod and Michael G. Dolence. "Concepts for Reengineering Higher Education," *CAUSE/EFFECT* (Summer 1991): 10-17.

6. Grassmuck, "Some Research Universities Contemplate Sweeping Changes, Ranging From Management and Tenure to Teaching Methods,"A29.
7. Smallen et al., "What Will It Take to 'Get It' in Higher Education?," 14.
8. Sharon J. Rogers and Charlene S. Hurt. "How Scholarly Communication Should Work in the 21st Century," *The Chronicle of Higher Education* (18 October 1989): A56.
9. "Online Systems Dominate NACUBO Cost Reduction Awards," *Manage IT* (October 1991): 1.
10. Robert B. Kozma and Jerome Johnston. "The Technological Revolution Comes to the Classroom," *Change*, Volume 23, Number 1 (January/February 1991): 10-23.
11. EDUCOM, Educational Uses of Information Technology (EUIT) Program. *The Joe Wyatt Challenge: 101 Success Stories of Information Technologies in Higher Education.* Washington, DC: EDUCOM; 1991.
12. Robert W. Spencer, "'After' the Registration Revolution," *College & University* (Summer 1991), American Association of Collegiate Registrars and Admissions Officers, 209-212.
13. David L. Wilson, "High Cost Could Deny Big Computer Advance to Some Colleges," *The Chronicle of Higher Education* (4 December 1991): A1, A32.

Transformation and the Chief Information Officer

James I. Penrod

Introduction

The general expectation that major investments in information technology (IT) infrastructures would result in significantly enhanced broadbased productivity has not been realized. It is now believed that this lack of anticipated productivity is due to the fact that primarily *existing* business practices have been automated. Simply speeding up old processes cannot address their fundamental performance deficiencies. To meet the pressures of today's world, speed, quality, innovation, and service must be incorporated into new models; therefore, we must re-engineer basic business processes. Re-engineering is defined as using the power of modern information technology to radically redesign job descriptions, workflows, control mechanisms, and decision-structures to achieve dramatic improvements in performance. The process of re-engineering leads to transformation which has already begun in some segments of business and industry. It is now time for these same processes to be adopted by higher education.

In the early 1980s, the idea for a chief information officer (CIO) was introduced in conjunction with the concept for information resources management (IRM). By the end of the decade, approximately 150 CIOs could be identified in higher education in the United States. In just the last three years, that number has doubled. The role of the CIO as a senior executive in an organization is to serve as an information policy officer, coordinate information technology planning with institutional strategic planning, manage and/or coordinate the organization's information resources, and participate in the development of new information technology capabilities. An IRM approach shifts the organizational information perspective from an historic operational focus to a new strategic focus, emphasizing how IT can contribute to accomplishing the institutional mission. Thus, it is imperative for the CIO to be at the forefront of any transformation process.

Successful CIOs are characterized by strong communication and interpersonal skills, being good general managers, having technical competence, having vision in the usage of IT, being good negotiators and consensus builders, having a global institutional view, being leaders and planners, and demonstrating energy and perseverance. Such attributes are necessary for individuals who will have major involvement in re-engineering campuses.

The transformation process requires the understanding that IT is an enabling force in our world, just as the steam engine was at the beginning of the industrial age. It is not just another tool available for humankind to use as they see fit. Re-engineering also requires an institution to commit to a level of quality, responsiveness, and service to clients or customers well beyond that which has been delivered to date. To achieve such goals, people throughout the organization have to be empowered to act and then be held responsible for doing so. Administrative processes, beginning with the most fundamental assumptions, need to be re-examined and redesigned in light of the capabilities of IT. This will necessitate rewriting most procedures and many policies. It also means that job descriptions must be oriented toward outcomes rather than tasks. Bureaucracies will give way to networked organizations with fewer levels, better communication channels, more flexibility, quicker decision-making mechanisms, and an outcome orientation.

Re-engineering relies upon the existence of a sophisticated IT infrastructure for support. Minimally, the infrastructure should include an all-purpose, campus-wide network with a defined upgrade path, an integrated corporate database with access provided to a wide range of people, access to scholarly information including more and more full text as time passes, and competent technicians and application specialists in a variety of areas across the institution.

Support for the infrastructure will come from the IT unit, the library, and personnel in almost all academic and administrative departments across the campus. In a transformed organization, managers will be responsible for their own information resources in much the way they are responsible for their own people, budget, and space. Much of the necessary coordination in the new organization structures will come through formalized networks of knowledge workers who do much of their communication by electronic means such as e-mail, voice mail, fax, and electronic data interchange. Some of the networks may well include individuals outside the institution, e.g., vendors, suppliers, advocates, etc.

Campuses with a CIO at the executive officer level already have an institutional IT champion. Those without a CIO or where the CIO is not at a true policy level need an identified executive officer who is an IT champion to ensure a close coupling between organizational goals and IT objectives. One of the best ways to bring this about is by linking strategic planning and management for the campus directly with information resources management tactical plans. This will usually be coordinated by the CIO; however, it is important for the specific plans to be derived by administrators or faculty who are directly responsible for implementing the plan. The CIO can serve as a real facilitator for institutional change as part of the transformation process through the strategic planning and coordination role.

The IT unit must be one of the first on campus to be re-engineered, and the CIO must provide strong leadership for this to occur. A new organizational culture will need to support distributed networks, empower IT technicians and knowledge workers outside of the IT unit to be more intuitive and less rational/logical in decision-making, to have a person-centered versus a unit-centered focus, and to establish self-directed teams with an institution-wide membership. Part of the new culture will be an emphasis on quality and the use of techniques such as total quality management (TQM) to achieve and maintain much higher standards. The IT staff will need to be highly professional, innovative, and committed to envisioning and reaching for new horizons.

As an institutional change agent, the CIO will need to do several things in support of transformation. A very important function is to provide ongoing education to campus executives as to how IT is an enabling force behind re-engineering and how it can help them discharge their responsibilities. Part of the planning and management function of the CIO must be to ensure that systems campus-wide are integrated and designed to support executives and front-line knowledge workers as well as applications area specialists such as the controller, the registrar, etc. This not only supports the concept of a corporate database, it also encourages and nurtures the idea of information resources management as a corporate responsibility versus an IT unit responsibility. When such a perspective is accepted, the institution is near to the point where information truly becomes a corporate asset.

Finally, although there have been calls for partnerships between the library and IT units for several years, there are still relatively few successful examples to be found. Since only about ten percent of IRM type organizations contain both the library and the typical IT unit, it is important for CIO and librarian partnerships to be formed as a prerequisite to a serious campus transformation project. Both are major and influential players at or near the policy level of colleges and universities. Both have great interest in distributing scholarly information down to the desktop, building campus-wide networks connected to local area networks (LANs) and national networks, and providing campus-wide IT instruction and education. Some of the resultant re-engineering restructuring is very likely to impact both the librarian and the CIO. It seems highly possible that redesigned jobs could combine certain functions now carried out separately by IT unit and library personnel, and a new academic service unit might be defined which functions more efficiently and effectively in providing higher quality service. The CIO and the librarian joining together to lead such redefinition, redesign, and restructuring could provide a meaningful example for the rest of the campus in demonstrating the fruitful possibilities of transformation.

Increasing societal pressures on higher education to hold down costs and improve productivity, the critical role of colleges and universities in educating knowledge workers of the twenty-first century, and the re-engineering movement in business and industry work together to demand significant change, in this decade, for higher education. Re-engineering concepts provide a basis for transforming our institutions of learning into learning organizations that can continue to lead the world of higher education.

Introduction to Concepts

Re-engineering: A Process for Transformation

Despite the evolution in management theory from Theory X to Theory Y to Theory Z, the fundamental assumptions about management have not radically changed over the past fifty years. In simple, basic terms, a successful management paradigm has involved stating the goals of the enterprise or institution clearly and precisely; explicitly defining what needed to be done to accomplish the goals; translating the work requirements into expectations of the employees; communicating the expectations through job descriptions and work plans; and, evaluating the results. Subordinates who complied with the policy and procedures were rewarded and promoted, and those who did not were ignored or punished.[1]

During the past two decades, the processes and procedures that were derived over the years to ensure good management and administrative practice, have, almost universally, been automated. Commonly, there have been major expenditures, and in many cases significant proportions of operating budgets were allocated to build management information systems and to maintain the resultant hardware, software, networks, and the people who operate them.

In the last several years, in all segments of the workplace—mass-production manufacturing, service companies, and non-profit enterprises—the environment has changed. Constituents or customers have become increasingly dissatisfied, employee turnover has increased, sales have been disappointing, operating expenditures in non-profit institutions have risen dramatically, and productivity has increased slower than expected. The promise and expectations of automation, given the magnitude of investment, have been at best mixed, and in many cases profoundly disappointing. CEOs, boards, politicians, and the public have begun to ask: What is the problem? Will investments in computing and communications ever pay off? Can we still manage?[2]

Richard Nolan answers by noting that we are in the midst of a basic shift in our economy. The industrial economy is transitioning to an information or service economy. He points out that the fundamental theories and practices of modern management were devised during the last major transition from an agrarian economy to the industrial age. There are important lessons to be learned from studying that economic shift. First, there must be some underlying technology to drive the transition. The steam engine fueled the industrial revolution, and the integration of computing and communications is the enabling force for the information/service economy. Secondly, productivity gains require that the new technology be incorporated into the workplace *and* that the organizational structure for doing work be changed to take advantage of the new technology. Bureaucracy developed and grew from the industrial organizational model. Today a new organizational structure must evolve to support a networked society.[3]

Michael Hammer observes that the lack of anticipated productivity is largely due to the fact that *existing* business and administrative practices have been automated. Position descriptions, workflows, control mechanisms, and decision-making structures developed well before the capabilities of today's computerized networks could even be imagined, contain fundamental deficiencies that cannot be overcome by automating or speeding up the old processes dictated by them. The concepts of serial processing, efficiency, and control were primary elements of the industrial model. A model for an information/service economy should incorporate ideas related to parallel processing, speed, quality, service, and innovation. Therefore the time has come to "re-engineer" the basic business processes of the enterprise whether it is in business, industry, government, or education. Re-engineering involves making a critical re-examination of *all* basic assumptions about the way things are done in light of existing and emerging technological capabilities and the necessity of dramatically improving quality and service, then redesigning work processes based upon the new assumptions.[4]

To date, most of the focus on transformation has come from the business sector. The dawn of the decade of the 1990s, however, seems to have marked an awakening in higher education to this future-shaping topic. Along with other institutional types, a number of prominent, large, research universities have begun initiatives to restructure and/or downsize while improving services, to implement TQM into administrative processes, to change existing cultural norms, structures, behaviors, and systems, and to bring transformation through bureaucracy busting and an increased reliance on the technological infrastructure and architecture of the campus.[5]

The CIO: An Agent of Change

William Synnott appears to have coined the term "chief information officer" speaking at the INFO '80 Conference while referring to a new corporate officer charged with leadership responsibilities for information resources management in an enterprise. An IRM approach has a strategic focus, emphasizing how information technology can contribute to the accomplishment of an organization's mission. A CIO is a senior executive of an organization with involvement in institutional strategic planning, who has responsibility for information technology planning, provides leadership in developing information policy, manages or coordinates the organization's information resources, and oversees the development of new information systems capabilities.[6]

The number of CIO positions in colleges and universities grew from a handful in the early 1980s to an estimated 200 by the end of the decade. Typically the positions were created in environments where significant change was underway or planned in the near future. By the mid 1980s effective CIOs demonstrated characteristics of being articulate and capable of persuading others to embrace change, having patience, being good listeners, and being capable of change themselves—sometimes having to revise fundamental assumptions and patterns.[7]

This relatively new, policy-level position, often created primarily to deal with significant change brought by information technology, and charged with direct responsibility for IT planning while playing a key role in strategic planning for the institution, is in an ideal position to be a champion for re-engineering and a major force for transformation on campus. Indeed, colleges and universities with competent, respected CIOs should be in a much better position to move forward with a progressive transformation program than those without an IT policy officer.

It is critical to note that a CIO is not in a position to be *the* leader of a transformation movement. Given the broadbased magnitude of change necessary for an institution to transform, that role will usually be filled by the president or chancellor, and occasionally by a very influential provost or chief operating officer. In addition to the CIO, several other senior-level university officers will need to play meaningful roles. These include the chief financial officer, the primary planning officer, the librarian, the human relations officer, and the deans.

The State of the CIO in Higher Education

The data presented in this section are based upon two national surveys of CIOs in higher education. The first was conducted in spring 1989 and included 58 respondents from an identified population of 139 colleges and universities. The second was concluded in fall 1991 and had 139 respondents from an identified population of 266 institutions. The first questionnaire contained 40 fairly detailed questions. The second duplicated 12 questions from the 1989 survey.[8]

Characteristics of CIOs

In 1991 the prototype CIO was a white male in his late forties who had been in the CIO position for approximately three years. His title was associate/ assistant or vice president/provost/chancellor and he had an administrative background. His median salary was approximately $80,000/year in a public comprehensive or research university with an enrollment of about 12,500 students. He had management responsibility for administrative and academic computing and data and voice communications. The CIO typically reported to the executive vice president, provost, or another vice president.

Although the overall 1991 profile is quite similar to the 1989 profile, some differences stand out. The median salary dropped from $90,000/year to $80,000/year. There appears to be three causes for this: (1) most new CIO positions were created at the associate/assistant vice president/provost/ chancellor level; (2) the institutions creating CIO positions were smaller; and, (3) fewer new positions were in research universities.

The proportion of public institutions responding to the 1991 survey was significantly higher than the 1989 proportion (74 percent versus 55 percent). This very likely has to do with the fact that a higher proportion of private colleges and universities are smaller and, therefore, less likely to create a CIO position. (Note that in 1989 there were more CIOs in research universities than other types, and many of them were private.) It may also relate to a propensity among private institutions to be less likely to respond to questionnaires in general.

CIO characteristics important to re-engineering include: the level of the position in the organizational structure, the background of the individual, institutional commitment to strategic planning, CIO responsibilities for IT planning, and the makeup of the CIO organization. The position must be at a policy level with frequent interaction with the key campus decision makers for there to be maximum impact. Obviously, a direct reporting relationship to the president or chancellor is highly advantageous. The tendency in the past three years seems to be to create more CIO positions in colleges and universities at lower levels than was the case with earlier CIO appointments.

CIOs with good administrative skills and a broad background are likely to contribute more to a transformation effort than those who have come to their position from a technical background. Only 20 percent of respondents to the 1991 survey indicated a technical background. This is a slight increase over 1989 when 16 percent of the CIOs had technical roots. The 1989 survey indicated that just under 52 percent of the CIOs held academic rank, and slightly over 34 percent had tenure in an academic department as well as holding their administrative position. Such breadth of background is most useful in interacting with academic units.

CIO Titles

Title	1989 Count	1989 Pct	1991 Count	1991 Pct
Vice President/ Provost/Chancellor	25	43	40	29
Assistant/Associate Vice President/Provost/ Chancellor	19	33	48	35
Director	10	17	33	24
CIO	0	0	7	5
Other	4	7	8	6
Totals	58	100	136	99

Table 1. Note: Due to rounding errors, some percentage totals will not equal 100 percent.

Units Supervised by CIO

Unit	1989 Count	1989 Pct	1991 Count	1991 Pct
Administrative Computing	52	90	136	100
Academic Computing	50	86	121	89
Data Communication	56	97	133	98
Voice Communication	40	69	98	72
IT Planning	19	33	55	40
TV Services	16	28	27	20
Media Services	9	16	28	21
Library	9	16	13	10
Other	54	93	100	74

Table 2.

CIO Reporting Structure

Officer	1989 Count	1989 Pct	1991 Count	1991 Pct
President/Chancellor	24	41	41	30
Executive/Other VP	20	34	61	45
Provost/Academic VP	11	19	29	21
Other	3	5	5	4
Totals	58	99	136	100

Table 3.

A commitment to strategic planning can be a great help in transforming a campus. The 1991 survey indicates that 62 percent of campuses with CIO respondents had an institutional strategic plan and that 65 percent had IT plans. This corresponded to 1989 results of 43 percent for campuswide plans and 67 percent for IT plans. The significant increase in institutional strategic plans is a positive sign for transformation. Another positive indication for CIO involvement in transformation is a slight increase in the pro-

Institutional Type

	1989		1991	
Type	Count	Pct	Count	Pct
Research University	30	52	39	29
Comprehensive University	19	33	50	37
Liberal Arts College	4	7	21	15
Community College	2	3	18	13
Other	3	5	8	6
Totals	58	100	136	100

Table 4.

CIO Salary

	1989		1991	
Range	Count	Pct	Count	Pct
Under $65,000	6	10	27	20
$65,000 to 74,999	11	19	24	18
$75,000 to 84,999	9	16	26	19
$85,000 to 94,999	6	10	25	18
$95,000 to 104,999	13	22	8	6
$105,000 to 114,999	12	21	14	10
$115,000 and over	0	0	10	7
Not reported	1	2	2	1

Table 5.

Institutional Size

	1989		1991	
Range	Count	Pct	Count	Pct
Under 2,000	3	5	9	7
2,000 to 4,999	9	16	19	14
5,000 to 9,999	6	10	28	21
10,000 to 14,999	10	17	24	18
15,000 to 19,999	4	7	15	11
20,000 to 24,999	5	9	13	10
25,000 and over	21	36	28	21
Totals	58	100	136	102

Table 6.

portion of CIOs who are charged with management responsibility for IT planning (40 percent in 1991 versus 33 percent in 1989). It should be noted that this implies a dedicated position in the IT organization devoted to planning. In 1989, almost 80 percent of CIOs indicated that they personally were involved in campus-wide IT planning.

The makeup of the IT organization may help determine the magnitude of the role a CIO will play in campus transformation. In addition to the units which define a CIO function, the other units most frequently administered are: IT planning (40 percent), media services (21 percent), television services (20 percent), and institutional research (18 percent). IT planning, as already noted, is most significant but institutional research is also very important in the support of transformation.

CIO Background

Area	1989		1991	
	Count	**Pct**	**Count**	**Pct**
Administrative	28	48	58	43
Academic	22	38	43	32
Technical	8	14	27	20
Mixed	0	0	4	8
Totals	58	100	136	101

Table 7.

CIO Age

Range	1989		1991	
	Count	**Pct**	**Count**	**Pct**
Under 45	11	19	35	26
45 - 49	23	40	49	36
50 - 54	17	29	30	22
55 and over	7	12	22	16
Totals	58	100	136	100

Table 8.

Types of CIO Organizations

The 1989 survey indicated that there were three types of CIO organizations. There were those comprised of academic and administrative computing and a network unit. This type of organization was labeled "CIO." Organizations with all of these units plus others such as IT planning, media services, television, institutional research, etc. were called "IRM." Where two of the three units which defined a CIO type organization existed along with other IT or information resource units, the organization was designated "other." The proportional makeup was 29 percent CIO, 57 percent IRM, and 14 percent other. Although this breakdown is not directly available from the 1991 survey data, it appears as if the proportion of "other" organizations may almost have disappeared. Thus, individuals who call themselves CIOs in higher education are highly likely to administer a true CIO or IRM type organization and would be significantly involved in any institutional commitment to utilize IT to enhance services by re-engineering administrative processes.

CIO Gender

Gender	1989		1991	
	Count	**Pct**	**Count**	**Pct**
Male	54	93	126	93
Female	4	7	10	7
Totals	58	100	136	100

Table 9.

Institutional Control

Type	1989		1991	
	Count	Pct	Count	Pct
Public	32	55	100	74
Private	26	45	36	26
Totals	58	100	136	100

Table 10.

Years in CIO Position

Number	1989		1991	
	Count	Pct	Count	Pct
1	13	23	22	16
2	11	19	24	18
3	9	16	24	18
4	11	19	14	10
5	8	14	17	13
6	0	0	9	7
7	0	0	13	10
8	3	5	2	1
9	0	0	1	1
≥ 10	2	3	10	7
Totals	57	99	136	101

Table 11.

Existing Strategic Plans

Type	1989		1991	
	Count	Pct	Count	Pct
IT Plan	39	67	89	65
Institutional Plan	25	43	84	62

Table 12.

Types of CIOs

The 1989 survey also identified three types of CIOs:

> First are CIOs who are policy officers reporting to the president/chancellor or the chief operating officer (provost or executive vice president). Many times such individuals are also executive officers of the institution, have line responsibility for the majority of information technology resources in the college or university, and have policy control (through purchasing approval) for the remainder. They interact daily with executive officers and deans participating in a broad array of decision-making. The institution likely

regards information technology as a strategic resource, wishes to maintain at least a "near follower" information technology strategy, and has committed resources to do so. The organization type is IRM or CIO. Planning is valued throughout the institution and the CIO is responsible for maintaining a strategic plan for information technology. The institution has an executive-level policy committee and one or more operational committees which focus upon IRM issues.

The second type of CIO is also a policy officer, probably reporting to the provost or executive vice president, and may or may not be an executive officer. He or she has line responsibility for substantial information resources, but many times major information technology units report elsewhere. The institution is likely to be large and/or a major research university with a strong commitment to "leading edge" or "near follower" strategy. There is defined funding from the institution and the major schools. The CIO interacts often with executive officers and deans, is expected to provide vision and leadership (probably through a meaningful planning process) but does not have policy control of information resource purchasing. The organization type is CIO or a limited IRM. An executive-level policy committee that may appoint ad hoc committees to deal with needed operational issues (where there is no standing operational committee) provides oversight for information technology.

Finally, there are CIOs who are senior administrators who may or may not be policy officers but usually are not institutional executive officers. They are not likely to often interact with executive officers except when there are difficulties or at budget time. They may be regarded as "hired guns" responsible for fixing problems with academic and administrative computing, data processing, and phone operations so that the executive officers do not have to worry about these areas. The institutional strategy toward information technology is undefined or "don't ask for a Cadillac if we can make do with a Yugo." It is unlikely that an institutional plan exists, but an information technology plan is desired. The plan and the process for deriving it are the total responsibility of the CIO. There is likely a joint policy and operational committee for information resources with some influential faculty representation. The organization

type may be IRM, CIO, or other, but unit groupings may be
more dependent upon historical culture than on an information management rationale.[9]

There is nothing in the 1991 survey data that would indicate that this
topology should be substantially revised. Either of the first two CIO types
could play meaningful roles in a transformation effort. Happily, the colleges
or universities most likely to engage in a transformation effort fit these scenarios and not the third one.

The Basic Elements of Re-engineering

IT: An Enabling Force

As Nolan observed, transformation cannot occur without some technology as
a driving force, and the integration of computing and communications is the
impetus behind the shift to an information/service economy. Hammer was
more pointed in noting that the capabilities of information technology must
be used as a shaping input, not as an implementation tool for re-
engineering.[10]

The idea that IT is more than a tool, that it makes possible the complete re-examination and substantial revision of the basic assumptions underlying all administrative processes and procedures is difficult for many to accept. But it is this concept which opens the door to empowerment, and the
other radical changes that transformation can bring to an enterprise.

Quality, Responsiveness, and Service

Much of the early literature focusing on TQM, statistical process control
(SPC), market-driven quality, etc., was developed to address growing concerns about productivity growth in the manufacturing sector. As new and
complex as quality improvement issues in manufacturing are, they are perceived to be not only different but vastly more complex in service enterprises
such as colleges and universities. Consequently, it is not enough to direct efforts toward "doing quality." The real change comes from creating environments, especially in service areas, where all the people in the organization are
dedicated to "being quality."[11]

For far too long, in the administrative areas of many colleges and
universities, particularly large public institutions, front-line employees have
been urged to "do their jobs," meaning to carry out the tasks defined in their
perspective position descriptions. The time has come where that emphasis
must change. All employees should strive to provide the best service possible

to campus constituents. This translates into timely, responsive actions to meet service needs, and producing reliable, error-free, quality documents or information for clients. Client or customer satisfaction, in the service arena, is said to equal the ratio of performance to expectations. The enterprises that best meet or exceed client or customer expectations, typically are those that communicate extensively. Communication is beneficial by showing clients (students) that the campus is attempting to articulate problems and issues rather than just react to them, and that there are real efforts to learn about and, where possible, to modify expectations the clients might have about service. Helping to mold expectations is not the same as manipulation. The purpose is to help the client to understand what they are receiving, to relate the service to their needs, and to understand what constitutes completely satisfactory service. An organizational commitment to undertake the effort to understand the needs and expectations of clients or customers helps to establish the conditions of superior performance.[12]

Empowered People

If employees are to strive to provide the best service possible to clients, they must be empowered to do so. Empowerment involves significant organizational changes as well as changes in the behavior of individuals. Traditionally, organizations emphasize a top-down, high control orientation that stresses clarity of roles, levels or authority, and the need for self-control and discipline. In an organization that empowers people, there is a belief that the most trustworthy source of authority comes from within the individual. Thus, the task of administration is to help people trust their own instincts in providing service and to take responsibility for the success of the organization.

In an empowered environment, individuals learn to count success in terms of contribution and service to customers, clients, and other units. They also learn that meaningful work, the opportunity to learn, and the chance to grow through one's own efforts is rewarding. In such an environment, administrators should let people know where they stand, share information and control, and take reasonable risks. Initially, this may require courage, but it will minimize the belief that one must be calculating and controlling to move up in the organization. Finally, empowerment means emphasizing autonomy over dependency in employees. That reduces fear, and demands that individuals take responsibility for their own actions.[13]

Process Redesign

The redesign of work processes requires making new assumptions about the way things are done. Hammer suggests seven principles to follow in examining assumptions and redesigning processes. (1) Capture information once and at the source. With today's networks and relational databases this is relatively easy to do and results in compressing the linear functions built into existing processes. (2) Organize fundamental processes and job descriptions around outcomes, not tasks. This often results in collapsing responsibilities for a function into a single unit or person. (3) Ensure that those who use the output of a process perform the process. When people closest to a process perform it, the overhead of administering it is substantially reduced. (4) Subsume or meld information processing functions into the traditional functions that produce the information. This disputes assumptions about specialized labor and that people are incapable of acting on information they generate. (5) Link parallel activities while in process rather then integrating the results. IT capabilities make it possible to link and coordinate parallel functions in process rather than at completion. (6) Treat geographically dispersed resources as though they were centralized. Databases, networks, and standardization permit the benefits of scale and coordination of centralization while maintaining the flexibility and service of decentralization. And, (7) put the decision point where the work is performed and build control into the designed processes. This requires that individuals be empowered with necessary authority and be held accountable for results.[14]

Restructuring

Over the past two decades, cost-plus pricing, the administrative lattice, and the academic ratchet have had dramatic impacts on many colleges and universities. Cost-plus pricing relies on price setting as a primary means to finance all programs at current levels after inflation (cost), and to fund new initiatives requiring augmentation (plus). The administrative lattice refers to the increase in staff (sixty percent between 1975 and 1985), the transfer of tasks to staff from faculty, the growth of consensus management, and the increase of costs coupled with a decline of efficiency as bureaucracy extends within an institution. The academic ratchet refers to the advance of an independent, entrepreneurial spirit among faculty leading to increased emphasis on research, publication, and teaching one's specialty rather than general introduction courses, often at the expense of coherence in an academic curriculum. Today some academic leaders are calling for a basic shifting of priorities along with substantial administrative redesign to combat these trends. They want their institutions to be not just learned, but more flexible, more able to focus their investments, and simpler in organization and management. They advocate growth by substitution, the recognition that resources are finite, and that growth in one area requires a corresponding reduction in another.[15]

Such institutional restructuring would endeavor to tear down the bloated bureaucracy, empower individuals at lower levels, reduce deferring routine decision-making to executive levels, reduce paperwork, regulations and procedures, encourage teamwork and collaboration within and across units and reward contributions to institutional goals thus reducing the tendency toward parochialism.[16]

The resulting "network" organization likely will have fewer levels of administration, fewer mid-managers, more knowledge workers (perhaps as much as 90 percent of the workforce in higher education), better communication channels, and a coordinated strategic visioning and management process. It will also rely upon the IT infrastructure and the corporate database(s) as the central nervous system for the enterprise.

The IT Infrastructure

Networks: Electronic and Human

The technological revolution in microprocessors has spurred the growth of high-performance, high-speed networks, multi-tasking network servers, graphical user interface (GUI) based desktop systems, high-performance relational database management systems, and gateway or linkage technology that permits these network-based systems to be connected to host computers, thus permitting access to the information tied up in mainframe systems. Such networks provide effective ways to supply access and data analysis capabilities to information in centralized systems for all knowledge workers who need such access to improve service. GUI provides a far more "user friendly" environment for these knowledge workers than can be supplied by mainframe application, thus enabling better responsiveness. Direct, unfiltered access by executives and by front-line workers to information previously derived through mid-managers will almost certainly prove to be beneficial to both groups. Finally, networked client/server computing can be used to redesign and re-engineer administrative processes without having to completely overhaul mainframe application systems.[17]

The electronic infrastructure is only part of networking. A formal network might encompass alliances and joint ventures with other organizations (educational entities, vendors, etc.), informal ties among internal administrators, teams that work across functions, and new ways of sharing information by using telecommunication infrastructures, management information systems, and other information technologies. Networks will truly matter to the campus when they affect patterns of relationships and change the frequency, intensity, and honesty of dialogue among network members on specific priorities.[18]

The Corporate Database

Institutions that are serious about transformation need a corporate database and need to provide broadbased access to it. The systems architecture will depend upon many factors including what is currently in place and what resources are available to make it more accessible. Some common database characteristics which need to be considered include: (1) easily accessible up-to-date summary information that relates to senior-level decision-making; (2) easily usable programs which allow exploration of successively greater levels of detail from the summary level down to data elements; (3) longitudinal comparison data; (4) integrated subsystems which accommodate cross-functional analysis; (5) routine operational reports available online; (6) operational reports and access mechanisms designed to support client/customer service by front-line knowledge workers; (7) reasonably straightforward *ad hoc* retrieval and report generation capabilities; and (8) the capability to do *ad hoc* statistical analysis on subsets of the database.[19]

Any discussion of a corporate database for a college or university today must include the idea of scholarly access to information needed for research, scholarship, and creative activities. The dream of building an electronic library is more than 20 years old, but is only now becoming a partial reality. The same networking and client/server technology described earlier coupled with relatively low-cost electronic and optical storage are enabling substantial electronic databases to be built and made available to scholars at their desktops.

Support for the Infrastructure

The CIO organization should facilitate the campus-wide planning process for IT, provide primary operation and maintenance for the backbone infrastructure, and provide appropriate campus-wide enterprise support functions. To facilitate planning, the CIO should ensure alignment between institutional strategy and IT strategies; ensure that IT is strategically considered by various campus units, develop through campus-wide consultation, strategic and tactical IT plans, and develop an operational plan for core IT functions and resources.

The campus-wide backbone IT infrastructure consists of voice, data, and image networks, links to regional, national, and global networks, and the strategic repository of data for institutional decision-making and scholarly access. (The need for a close partnership between the CIO and the librarian on several of these issues is evident.) It is also the CIO's responsibility to coordinate policy, standards, and procedures which enable the integration of IT resources.

Campus-wide enterprise support functions incorporate such things as the following: core facilities (general usage machines, labs, the backbone network, etc.); maintenance, training, common software, etc.; leading edge technology, instructional development, facilities management; consultation with small units or on general issues; and, encouraging partnerships, joint development efforts, and innovative projects.

Infrastructure support needed at the administrative division, school, or departmental level will vary from institution to institution but typically would include such items as ensuring alignment between school or division IT plans and campus-wide strategic and tactical plans, operating local client/servers and LANs, ensuring observance of campus-wide standards, developing local or specialized applications, and contributing data and information to the enterprise repository.

It is important to reiterate the critical need for the CIO and the librarian to become partners in designing and implementing an information infrastructure to meet the needs of the twenty-first century. To do so implies joining together to provide campus leadership, hopefully by example, that demonstrates transformation principles in action for the benefit of all.[20]

The Institutional Role of the CIO

The IT Champion

An IT champion is a policy-level officer of the institution who understands the need for an IT/institutional strategy linkage and works with other policy officers to see strategies developed and implemented throughout the campus. CIOs at the vice president/chancellor level probably best fit this role, however, CIOs who are members of the president's/chancellor's council may also be quite successful in it. One of the primary functions of the IT champion is to ensure that the use of information technology to meet campus-wide strategic needs is discussed and understood by the policy group and that such discussions become routine. Another function is to align IT goals with institutional mission through a process of strategic planning and management. Finally, the CIO champion should encourage and nurture networks, consisting of people from various organizational levels, specifically designed to continually strengthen the IT/institutional linkage.[21]

A Facilitator of Change

Transformation requires significant and prolonged change. Some of the dimensions of change are as follows: (1) Role complexity will increase due to continuous changes in processes and organization. (2) Managers needs to cope with unclear lines of authority and decision-making will be heightened due to innovations such as matrix-management and self-directed work teams. (3) There will be increased skill requirements in a transformed environment. (4) Many problem-focused and outcome-oriented teams will be formed requiring different leadership and managerial abilities. (5) Changes in evaluation systems will be needed to assess individual, team, or unit success. (6) Cultural adjustments will be required due to changing accountability and authority. (7) Conventional planning processes will need to change, involving more people, shortening cycles, but focusing on longer term strategies. And, (8) changing the technology infrastructure will be a senior management priority enabling administrative and technology processes to be intertwined.[22]

Good CIOs are accustomed to holistic process thinking, and continual change has been evident throughout their professional lives, making them excellent candidates as facilitators for the kind of changes mentioned. While CIOs may facilitate the re-engineering process within administrative units, the unit managers should decide exactly what changes are made. As important a role as some CIOs may have, as previously stated, the CEO should begin the process, and it should be driven by the entire senior management team.[23]

The CIO and the IT Unit

Leadership

It is up to the CIO to encourage an attitude that views change as opportunity, and instill a "can-do" spirit into IT staff members, then to see that these ideas become cultural values. One method to bring this about suggests using developmental stages. In stage one, the leader strikes a bargain with followers where something is provided to the followers that they want in exchange for something the leader wants. In the second stage, the leader provides a climate and interpersonal support that enhances followers' opportunities for fulfillment of needs for achievement, responsibility, competence, and esteem. Stage three has the leader and followers developing a set of shared values and commitments that bond them together in a common cause. Finally, the leader institutionalizes improvement gains into the everyday life of the organization, thereby ensuring that they become part of the organizational culture. This requires turning the improvements into routines so that they become second nature and are passed on as "values" to others. It also demands that the values be guarded, reinforced, and introduced to new members of the organization.[24]

As this model implies, leadership for transformation is different than traditional notions. Instead of being solely a function of position on an organization chart, leadership will be determined by an individual's knowledge and expertise on a project-by-project basis. Leaders will be found throughout a networked organization, and the IT unit will need to have several people capable of assuming leadership on given issues.

Culture

One important aspect of transformation is a change in organizational culture. If a CIO is to play a major role in re-engineering, a new culture must be introduced into the IT unit early on in the process. The professional management culture that exists in most IT units (and other administrative units) will give way to one of entrepreneurialism. Such a shift contrasts several dimensions moving from: (1) external controls to internal controls, (2) conformity to rules to creativity within bounds, (3) central control to individual autonomy, (4) rational/logic decision-making to intuitive decision-making, (5) centralized systems to distributed networks, (6) vertical hierarchies to horizontal networks, (7) adult-child to adult-adult professional relationships, and (8) organization-centered to person-centered focus.[25] It is important to understand that these shifts occur within the context of empowerment as discussed earlier. That is to say that individuals are encouraged to make decisions and act based on goals of providing the best possible service to constituents, not on parochial interests.

Standards

IT units have long advocated standards, but, in fact, relatively few colleges and universities have campus-wide standards that come close to those found in many businesses. The reason usually given for this centers on issues of academic freedom. In reality it is much more related to results from the academic ratchet and a focus on allegiance to a particular unit, as opposed to interest in the good of the whole.

Creating and implementing meaningful institutional standards are prerequisites to building and operating an IT infrastructure that can support re-engineering and transformation. As client/server administrative applications expand (and they will), and as more and more academic and administrative functions blend together, this becomes even more important.

Such standards cannot be dictated by the CIO. Rather, they need to be derived through the strategic planning process and reviewed on an ongoing basis. In an integrated networked environment, far more coordination will be necessitated between connected units than has ever been true before.

New Horizons

In many ways, one of the most important roles of a CIO is that of being a catalyst for change. Exercising that role within the IT unit will significantly contribute to the unit's capability to support transformation. It might not be a bad idea for the IT unit to serve as a pilot testing ground for transformational changes. It is a natural candidate for early application of networked organizational structure, a shift of organizational culture, a more client/service centered orientation, productivity enhancement methodologies such as TQM and self-directed work teams, the empowerment of all staff members, and redesign of position descriptions and administrative processes to focus on outcomes versus tasks. IT staff will, therefore, need to continually look to new horizons and recognize that they need to go where they have not gone before.

Supporting Transformation

Executive Education

Seeing that there are useful discussions among senior administrators regarding strategic usage of IT is one function of a CIO and is a powerful means of executive education. Having an understanding of strategic and policy issues, however, is not enough. Transformation will move faster if senior administrators use such things as voice mail, electronic mail, executive information systems, electronic filing for documents, etc. In most cases, two levels of education and training will be necessary for this to be accomplished.

First, it is crucial to train the executives' staff to use these features of an IT infrastructure. That training probably should be tailored to a given office or a suite of very similar offices (all vice presidents). A well-trained and experienced office staff can answer questions that will surely arise on-the-spot by the executive and, if they become enthusiastic systems users, they may provide motivation for the executive to learn and use these capabilities.

Second, the executives need to be educated for hands-on use. These sessions should include executives only and, if possible, be conducted by someone special (a professional from outside the institution or a senior-level internal resource). Although time for such activities will not be easy to schedule, the training should not be rushed. Executives' use of the IT infrastructure can provide a tremendous behavioral example to the institution.

Information: A Corporate Asset

The IRM concept and the initial definition of a CIO was built around the idea that information is an asset. An asset is defined as "anything owned that has exchange value." Accountants, however, define an asset as "something . . . carried on the books . . . on the basis that it represents either a property right or value acquired . . . ." Thus, inventory is an asset. Information is the same sort of asset. One of the jobs of a CIO or a librarian is to collect information that has value, so that someone will "buy," i.e. use it. The more people who find information stored in an institution's data repository of value, the greater the corporate asset.[26] A primary function of the CIO is to manage the IT infrastructure so that information is treated as an asset.

As a corporate asset, information and data elements from which it may be derived should: (1) be safeguarded and be reliable, and (2) be accessible by as many people who can beneficially use it (therefore further increasing its value). Obviously, information resource units have great responsibility for the reliability and safekeeping of information. But, as systems become more and more distributed, a broad array of offices also must assume similar responsibilities. The design of the infrastructure and the policies governing security and use control access. The CIO needs to be an advocate for access by all who have a "need to know" so that the service provided may be continually improved.

Communication Channels

The broadly defined networks described earlier may provide some of the best communication channels for transformation in the institution. The social architecture is the foundation of such networks and of meaningful communication.

Social architecture refers to the mechanisms through which key members make trade-offs, and to the flow of information, power, and trust that shapes how the trades get made. For a network to be effective as designed, senior management must drive the process of building the appropriate social architecture. There are three important steps in doing this. First, the network must be designed. A basic objective is to find the right mix of individuals whose organizational understanding, personal motivations, and functional expertise allow them to produce the expected outputs within specified time frames. Second, senior management must deal with mismatches when the performance of members whose behaviors hurt the network becomes visible. Networks will tend to bring to the forefront informal leaders with exceptional competence and to reveal individuals who cannot make the change to do business in this new way. The social architecture will break down if problem people are not removed from the network. Finally, an intense and sustained focus on the fundamentals of organizational mission and goals rather than on more abstract concepts is necessary. This is not to say that appeals to culture, teamwork, or values are not important to the organization, but that the purposes of networks are to develop professional trust and to enhance understanding of the specifics of the business.[27]

In addition to networks, more traditional communication channels should also be used to support transformation. The strategic and tactical planning process provides a very effective means of communication. The advisory committee structures that are common in CIO organizations can be utilized with good results. Special task forces are also quite effective in colleges and universities. Finally, periodic reports, formal statements, and memorandums of encouragement from senior administrators, including the CIO, can be most useful forms of communicating expectations.

IT: A Corporate Responsibility

CIOs who become involved in a transformation effort will work to involve far more people across the campus in the planning and management process for IT. They will implement distributed networks, client/servers, and data repositories throughout the various organizational units of the college or university. They will coordinate the creation of policy and procedures that distribute responsibilities for the operation and management of IT functions formerly centralized in computer centers. Within the IT unit, they will create self-directed work teams that will, over time, manage themselves. In short, CIOs will help to build an environment where administrators in all units begin to manage IT resources in ways similar to their management of other resources such as money and space. In a transformed organization, information technology will truly be a campus-wide responsibility.

Since the creation of the CIO position, there have been those who call for its elimination. This change in distribution of activities described above, whether led by a CIO or not, has lead to more speculation that the CIO was a position never needed or one that shortly will outlive its usefulness.[28] Such speculation completely misses the point for the creation and somewhat rapid growth of CIOs in higher education and other sectors. The CIO position is rapidly evolving toward the same type of position as chief financial officer (CFO), and as the recognition grows that information is indeed a corporate asset and that IT management is a corporate responsibility, the ranks of CIOs will continue to grow, not fade away.

The CIO, Transformation, and the Library

Distributing Scholarly Information

Both CIOs and librarians should be committed to building and maintaining an infrastructure supporting transformation that maximizes access and utilization of faculty and student scholars. That will require a wide range of information and knowledge resources in the complete array of formats in which they are produced. Such resources may reside locally or some far distance from the campus. It is therefore necessary for CIOs and librarians to strive to work together, perhaps in synergistic leadership roles, in developing and implementing network strategies for the institutions they serve that will bring such capabilities to workstations on the desktop.

Local area networks serving specific units, a wide area network serving the entire campus, and links to national networks such as the soon to be developed National Research and Education Network (NREN) provide the electronic roadways for the information/service economy. Building such roadways may take a decade or longer to complete. Perhaps just as important as constructing the infrastructure is the provision of the education and training necessary to navigate this new terrain. Both IT units and libraries have major (and growing) roles to play in providing the needed education and consultation.

An Alliance for Progress

Only ten percent of IRM type organizations contain both IT units and the library. Thus, it is imperative for CIOs and librarians to form an alliance for progress that goes beyond friendly cooperation if the major information resource organizations on campus are to support transformation in the most significant ways possible. There are several initiatives that might forge such an alliance: (1) CIOs could move to include librarians in more significant ways in network planning; (2) CIOs and librarians could define networks of staff members from each unit and charge them with responsibilities to begin to address specified scholarly access issues; (3) they could work together to survey perceived needs and issues of concerns from academic departments; (4) they could set up communication channels where information from their respective national professional organizations, vendor contacts, colleagues, etc. is shared with key decision makers in both units; and, (5) most importantly, they could examine ways to restructure their organizations from a re-engineering perspective to provide services to clients in the most efficient and effective ways possible.

This could well mean moving current functions from one unit to another, or combining parts of units from each area into a newly defined service unit. Obviously, this would require an objective stepping away from territorial concerns (something that few CIOs or librarians have done to date) and concentrating on the needs of the clients above all else. But that is exactly what transformation is all about! Such an example could make a very bold and lasting statement to a campus about the fundamental meaning of transformation, and about the quality of leadership of the CIO and librarian.

Concluding Remarks

Higher education will be forced to find an acceptable response to the pressures of increasing costs, flat or decreasing funding, heightened constituent expectations, and reaction to rapid environmental changes. Colleges and universities absolutely must break the mold of the administrative lattice and academic ratchet. The re-engineering process offers a context for a thorough reexamination of the assumptions about the way things are done in higher education. It can easily encompass and enhance new paradigms which are already underway. A commitment to true transformation requires institutional analysis far more critical and complex than that required by an accreditation visit, resource redistribution more extended than any caused by fiscal crisis, and broadbased restructuring beyond any resulting from a systems merger. Even moderate results, however, by the measurement standards of transformation could be far reaching, and almost assuredly would have as much impact on academics as it would on administrative functions.

In considering a transformation commitment, colleges and universities must understand the consequences of maintaining the status quo while the rest of the world changes. Without a significant shift by higher education, the confidence of constituents and the general public will, in all probability, continue to erode, financial pressures will continue to build resulting in a permanent loss of quality, and the future leaders of the society will not be educated as well as they might be to cope with the challenges of the twenty-first century.[29]

The process of re-engineering the workplace of academia requires "thinking big," extraordinary commitment, and absolute dedication to the accomplishment of the institutional mission. It will, however, drive transformation and move higher education fully into the era of an information/service economy. It certainly is not a consideration for those weak of heart, but it could well be a path for maintaining the best and most successful system of advanced learning in the world.

Notes

1. Thomas J. Sergiovanni, "Leadership and Preparing Educational Leaders," The Mary Ann Alia Distinguished Lecture, California State University, Los Angeles, School of Education, September 24, 1991.
2. James I. Penrod and Michael G. Dolence, *Re-engineering a Process for Transforming Higher Education*, Professional Paper Series, #9, CAUSE (Boulder, CO, 1992): 1.
3. Richard L. Nolan, "Too Many Executives Today Just Don't Get It!," *CAUSE/EFFECT* (Winter 1990): 5-11.
4. Michael Hammer, "Re-engineering Work: Don't Automate, Obliterate," *Harvard Business Review* (July-August 1990): 104-112.
5. Karen Grassmuck, "Some Research Universities Contemplate Sweeping Changes, Ranging from Management and Tenure to Teaching Methods," *The Chronicle of Higher Education*, 12 September 1990, (Article A1, A29-A31); Gardner, Catherine, Timothy R. Warner, and Rick Biedenweg, "Stanford and the Railroad," *Change*, November/December 1990, 23-27; *Sustaining Excellence in the 21st Century: A Vision and Strategies for the University of California's Administration*, Report and Recom-

mendations, March 1991; and, *Transforming Administration at UCLA: A Vision and Strategies for Sustaining Excellence in the 21st Century*, August 1991.

6. James I. Penrod, Michael G. Dolence, and Judith V. Douglas, *The Chief Information Officer in Higher Education*, Professional Paper Series, #4, CAUSE (Boulder, CO, 1990): 1.

7. Judith A. Turner, "As Use of Computers Sweeps Campuses, Colleges Vie for Czars to Manage Them," *The Chronicle of Higher Education* (30 May 1984, 1): 14.

8. Penrod, Dolence, and Douglas, 1-39; Charles R. Thomas, "Chief Information Officers in Higher Education," CIO Special Interest Group, CAUSE 91 (December 4, 1991): 1-14.

9. Penrod, Dolence, and Douglas, 21-22.

10. Michael Hammer, "Re-engineering Your Business," AT&T Computer Systems Symposium, April 2, 1990.

11. Jeff Hallett and Kris Hefley, "The Great Quality Mystery," *The Present Futures Report* (November 1991): 5.

12. Hallett and Hefley, 5.

13. Peter Block, *The Empowered Manager* (San Francisco: Jossey-Bass, 1987): 20-24.

14. Michael Hammer, "Reengineering Work: Don't Automate, Obliterate," *Harvard Business Review* (July-August 1990): 110-112.

15. Robert Zemsky and William F. Massy, "Cost Containment, Committing to a New Economic Reality," *Change* (November/December 1990): 22.

16. Charles E. Young, Introduction Letter, *Transforming Administration at UCLA: A Vision and Strategies for Sustaining Excellence in the 21st Century*, August 1991.

17. James I. Penrod, Peter P. Quan, and Chris Rapp, "Distributing EIS Through Networks," *Developing Executive Information Systems for Higher Education* (San Francisco: Jossey-Bass, 1992), in press.

18. Ram Charan, "How Networks Reshape Organizations—For Results," *Harvard Business Review* (September-October 1991): 104-105.

19. Penrod and Dolence, 50-51

20. James M. Rosser and James I. Penrod, "Computing and Libraries: A Partnership Past Due," *CAUSE/EFFECT* (Summer 1990): 24.

21. Penrod and Dolence, 48-49.

22. John F. Rockart and James E. Short, "The Networked Organization and the Management of Interdependence," *The Corporation of the 1990s: Information and Organizational Transformation* (New York: Oxford University Press, 1991): 212-215.

23. Allan E. Alter, "The Corporate Make-Over," *CIO* (December 1990): 34.

24. Thomas J. Sergiovanni, "Adding Value to Leadership Gets Extraordinary Results," *Educational Leadership* (May 1990): 23-24.

25. Peter S. Delisi, "Lessons from the Steel Axe: Culture, Technology, and Organizational Change," *Sloan Management Review* (Fall 1990): 86.

26. Gerald M. Hoffman, "Is Information an Asset?" *Information Management Forum* (December, 1990): 3.

27. Penrod and Dolence, 19.

28. Ralph Carlyle, "The Out of Touch CIO," *Datamation* (August 15, 1990): 30-34; and Peter Krass, "Managing Without Managers," *Information Week* (November 11, 1991): 44-51.

29. Penrod and Dolence, 43.

Chief Information Officers, Academic Libraries, and the Information Job Family

Anne Woodsworth and Theresa Maylone

Introduction

It is commonly accepted that the rapid infusion of information technology into colleges and universities is bringing computing centers, libraries, and telecommunications operations closer together. On some campuses, this integration has led to administrative merging of libraries with computing centers and other "information partners." Even where there is no operational merger, the influence of a Chief Information Officer (CIO) on the library is often critical to the success of the library and vice versa. The degrees of influence of a CIO can range from total control to unobtrusive yet real power being exerted that can affect a library's mission as well as its ability to fulfill it.

Even without an actual administrative merger, the successes of academic libraries and academic computing centers are inextricably bound together. At the same time as CIO positions emerged in colleges and universities, there was an infusion of information technologies into the fabric of campus life that lead to the work of librarians and other information service providers on campus becoming "informated." As a result, work is no longer readily identifiable as naturally belonging either in the library or the computing center or other like units.

A current study of jobs in both environments has provided information on the similarities among jobs in libraries and academic computing centers and the extent to which they might belong to a single job family rather than two or more traditionally separate ones. The study found a bell curve: a small number of jobs that are identical, many that were similar in part, and another small number in which there were no similarities. Although the study was done on campuses where CIO positions existed, the study pointed to the need for more, closer and better coordination of at least two of the information partners on campus—libraries and academic computing. In short, if CIOs and librarians aim to become partners they must, in the future, pay more at-

---

© by Anne Woodsworth.

tention to other "I" words—viz. the development of a policy and reward *In*-frastructure that supports and rewards *I*ntegration. Without more emphasis on these, the people responsible for operating the *I*nformation systems are unlikely to participate in the transformation and re-engineering described in other chapters in this volume. This chapter discusses the emergence of CIO positions as a result of the integrating technologies, their influence on academic libraries, and the impact of diffusion of information technologies on jobs at levels below the CIO.

Gale-Force Winds of Change

The two previous chapters in this volume speak to the current dramatic transformation that is in order for higher education, and, along with them, transformation of our world of libraries, information systems, services, transmission, or resources. Whether you consider information as an entity or a process (Buckland, 1991), the need for transformation on all fronts is apparent. Perhaps more than any others, academic libraries, academic computing centers, and their parent organizations, are essentially agents that deal with the total university of knowledge-information interaction: information-as-knowledge, information-as-process, and information-as-thing. The nature of their business makes them only too aware of the dramatic changes that have and are occurring in this field alone. The winds that influence these changes appear to be building to gale force.

For example, in the world of education for library and information studies, these changes have wrought much agonizing discussion about what the field of librarianship is, what it should be called, and what the future information professional will be doing. Let's spend a few minutes illustrating the kinds of tornadoes and hurricanes that are buffeting the educational side of the field, apart from the technological maelstrom:

- *There is uncertainty about the value systems that have provided our educational institutions with their Good Housekeeping seals of approval.* The process and criteria for accreditation of institutions of higher education are being questioned at many levels—by the federal government, by many states, and by colleges and universities themselves. Specialized accreditation agencies, including the one administered by the American Library Association, are under attack by administrators in colleges and universities as well as by their own professions. The values that underlie the standards as well as the processes of accreditation are being buffeted by questions about costliness, validity, and value to the institution.

- *There is open acknowledgement of the need to transform the profession.* An independent and unaffiliated group calling itself the Strategic Visions Steering Committee (independent and unaffiliated group) has grown out of a free-wheeling electronic discussion on BITNET in 1991. The group is trying to encourage broad discussions on listservers and at meetings with a view to transformation of the profession. It is hoped that the eddies of action stimulated by the group will mount to large-scale grass roots change. In January 1992, the American Library Association announced plans to mount a research project (Project Century 21) to investigate future directions of the profession. Both projects are indicators of recognition that transformation is imminent, if not already occurring. Of the two, the action agenda planned by the Strategic Visions Steering Committee holds most promise of influencing change in a profession that is already half-way through a transformation, the process for which will be demonstrated later in this chapter.

- *Our depressed economy is forcing a shrinkage and amalgamation that is unprecedented in the field of higher education.* The saga of program closures, mergers of departments and schools is familiar to the library and information science professions. Whole colleges and universities are closing or teetering on the brink of bankruptcy. Stories appear regularly in the daily press as well as the *Chronicle of Higher Education* about measures being taken by colleges and universities to meet shortfalls in revenue. Some are traumatic to librarians (e.g. closure of the library school at Columbia University); others are almost humorous (e.g. the University of Maine's sale of its prize herd of Jersey cows). Within academic support units such as libraries and academic computing, the budget squeeze is inexorable. The resulting "transformations" to the information infrastructure as we know it today may happen faster than any of those affected may care to accept. Hence, it is critical to anticipate the tornadoes before they hit. Organizational mergers of related units, outsourcing of library and computing support services, outright elimination of some information technology operations, forced decentralization of information and computing services, and total refocusing of goals and service orientations are among the measures that can be contemplated. In the past decade, libraries and computing centers have had the luxury of being information islands gradually "drifting" together. The experience and lessons learned can perhaps point to solutions as the need to transform both units becomes acute.

These are only a few of the winds around us. The changing technologies themselves and the rapid appearance of new generations of increasingly powerful hardware and software, are paramount, of course. Other societal trends that affect us include the demand for more creativity, autonomy, and quality at work, particularly at professional and managerial levels (Drucker, 1988). The 1980s also saw flattening of organizations and massive reductions in the number of middle managers, particularly in the corporate sector (Bignell, 1989; Byrne, 1988). While this does not appear to have occurred in higher education as yet, fiscal pressures may force this sector to review the need for mid-level managers, in which case the question of whether library and academic computing center directors are considered middle managers would need to be addressed.

In short, there are enormous precedents and pressures to rethink what libraries and computing services do, how they do it, and how they are positioned and operated with the institution. Not only is the relationship between these two organizations at issue, but so is the management structure of the academy, the working relationships of its information providers, and of course, the skills and knowledge needed to perform the work itself.

Therefore, the mandate for educators in the field of library and information science is to anticipate the transformational issues and to make dramatic and far-reaching changes in not just how they educate, but what they educate for. Just as professionals in libraries and computing centers need to restructure their work and their organizations, so will it be necessary for educators to know what the information professions will be throughout, and at the end, of their transformation. Without that knowledge, colleges and universities cannot prepare the kinds of graduates that will be needed in the future. Educators also must become activists in the transformation discussed in this book.

The concept of "re-engineering" by James Penrod and Jane Ryland mentioned in earlier chapters is critical. However, to perform as change agents, all involved must understand the assumptions upon which the transformation will be based. Ryland and Penrod both alluded to the need to redesign work processes based upon new assumptions. Penrod, from the organizational perspective, provided assumptions about some of the organizational frameworks that allow colleges and universities to manage their information resources. These assumptions cannot be ignored. He demonstrated that CIOs are in place in approximately ten percent of our institutions of higher education and that ten percent of those had administrative responsibility for libraries. He asserted, and very rightly so, that:

> CIOs and librarians must form coalitions in order to build
> redesigned and improved information infrastructures so
> they can assist in the transformation that higher education

so critically needs, and in order to meet the needs of the twenty-first century (1992, p. 14).

While the need for CIOs (or other information service managers) to form coalitions is self-evident, the need for a CIO is not.

The 90 Percent View

As academic librarians (and other members of the information job family on campus) build a base of assumptions on which to shape the future, it is important to recognize that 90 percent of colleges and universities manage without a CIO at present. The traditional organizational structure of most colleges and universities has a library director reporting mostly to a provost or vice-president for academic affairs as shown in Figure 1.

In this configuration, administrative and academic computing usually report to a senior officer who is not responsible for the academic part of the institution. There are, of course, variations on this, with some institutions having an associate provost or director of academic computing who reports to

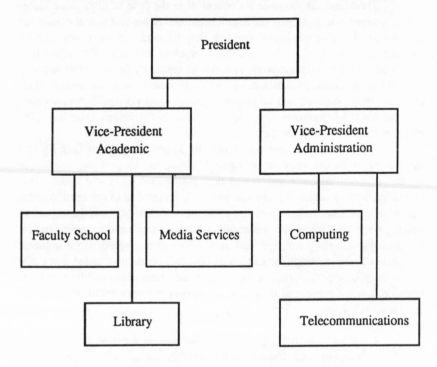

Figure 1. Traditional campus organization.

the same office as the library director. Impressionistic evidence indicates that this has been occurring more often in recent years.

When the first wave of CIOs appeared in both the corporate sector and higher education in the early 1980s, they reported to presidents, as shown in Figure 2.

It was almost by definition that CIOs reported to the Chief Executive Officer, both in the corporate sector (Brumm, 1989; Synnott and Gruber, 1981) and in higher education (Fleit, 1986; McCredie, 1983). However, in higher education at least, this is no longer the predominant model. More typical of late is a CIO position at the associate vice-presidential level, sometimes reporting to the same person as the library director, as shown in Figure 3.

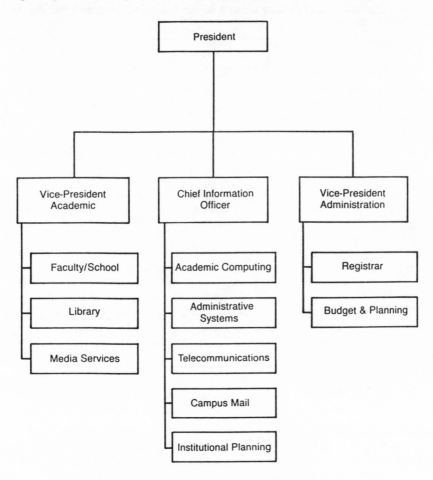

Figure 2. Early CIOs in higher education.

Although the position at this level might function and be considered to be a CIO, its relationship with the library is indirect and based on the kind of coalition mentioned by Penrod. Therefore, in building assumptions about the future, it is important to recognize that traditional organizational structures remain largely unchanged, while the nature of work at lower levels in the organization is being altered to include cross-functional, multi-skilled, and self-managed team approaches (Micossi, 1990).

As Penrod's survey indicated, CIO positions are still being established. Yet, the positions have lower salaries and lower reporting levels and appear to be more on a par with library director positions. Some position advertisements still convey a desire to want the CIO to do and be all. Note the comprehensive qualifications wanted in the following advertisement for an

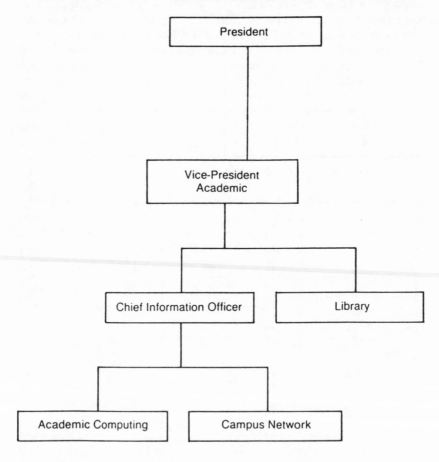

Figure 3. Typical CIO/library relationship in higher education.

Associate Vice President for Information Services for Potsdam College of the State University of New York:

> . . . candidates must demonstrate significant experience with both a library and a computer services organization and should have some knowledge of institutional research, telecommunications, and such other areas as might be appropriate. A Master's degree is required as is successful administrative experience, including management of personnel and budget in a multi-faceted service organization, strong oral and written communication skills, evidence of leadership exercised in an academic environment, and experience in planning. It is expected that the successful candidate will have had primary responsibility for an RFP development and/or contract negotiation, and a system installation, in one of the areas of responsibility. Experience in obtaining grants and corporate donations is desirable. Candidates should have a strong commitment to the importance of information technology in the education of citizens for life-long learning. They should enjoy the give-and-take of ideas in a positive environment of shared decision-making. A demonstrated commitment to affirmative action and diversity is imperative (Potsdam, 1991).

Perhaps this lengthy list is the reason why 90 percent of colleges and universities have yet to establish the positions—the credentials are daunting!

Seriously, there are many reasons why 90 percent of institutions of higher education do not establish CIO positions, and apparently function well without them. Some institutions achieve the desired planning, change, and transformation through team (or committee) structures that involve the key personnel who have responsibility for information resources on campus. Some settings may simply be too small for a full-time CIO. A CIO position might be perceived as signaling too much commitment and spending on technology. A campus environment might react negatively to the creation of a new senior (and presumably highly paid) administrator. Conceivably, presidents or vice presidents might feel that they have too many direct reports already. In addition, as the information technologies become distributed on campuses, responsibility for IT management will also be spread throughout the organization to the point that a number of mini-CIOs are needed, not just one. In short, institutions are now more prone to question the assumptions that, in the early 1980s, led to a wave of CIO positions being established.

Since the positions have been around long enough, some of the early myths surrounding them are being dispelled:

- *They are not omnipresent.* Only ten percent of colleges and universities have CIO positions.

- *They are not carnivorous.* Not all CIO positions encompass all IT functions on campus (Penrod, 1990) (Woodsworth, 1991).

- *They are not omnipotent.* Higher education is known for its diffused, sometimes seemingly chaotic, and negotiated decision-making processes. Therefore CIO positions are seldom sole decision makers about IT (Woodsworth, 1991).

- *They are not identical.* Their roles, responsibilities, and span of control vary enormously and are usually tempered by institutional politics and traditions (Woodsworth, 1991).

Finally, the past decade has also indicated that:

- *They are not everlasting.* A recent report indicates that a growing number of companies are eliminating the CIO and/or distributing their responsibilities to line management (Wilder, 1992).

Wilder's report in *Computerworld* is a telling one. Firstly, it echoes what Penrod's most recent 1991 survey indicated in this book: viz.—that CIOs are experiencing a downward shift in reporting levels and parallel title changes. The article discusses the results of an annual survey by Deloitte & Touche that found that 36 percent of companies had dismissed or demoted their CIO. Wilder points to three primary causes: corporate or centralized functions being downsized; authority for information systems functions being dispersed to units that are faster and more responsive to customer needs; and a return to the holding company mentality—all of which are stimulated by the economic recession.

If a common assumption holds—that trends in the corporate sector are echoed in the public sector—then it is not inconceivable that CIOs in higher education will experience similar reduction in their numbers in the next few years.

The pervasiveness of information technologies means that IT is no longer a novelty on campus. Information workers are doing jobs that may or may not be guided by the vision of a CIO. More importantly for academic libraries, the information resources jobs on our campuses are no longer readily identifiable as naturally belonging either in academic computing or the library, as indicated earlier.

Computers in Libraries, or Is It Libraries in Computers

At this stage in the evolution of information technology, the Computers in Libraries conference at which this study was originally presented might just as appropriately have been called "Libraries in Computers"! Mere word play or a trick of speech cannot possibly convey the complexity that results when computers and libraries are brought together—in whatever order. But as with so many simplistic phrases, this word trick has a little ring of truth that causes us to stop and think.

It was a similar nagging ring that led to a study[1] of the effect of the integration of information technologies in libraries and academic computing centers. With or without an administrative coupling that forced previously separate staffs to become more closely interconnected, the perception was that the work performed using the information technologies had altered radically, to the extent that work done in computing centers and in libraries could no longer be said to belong naturally in one unit or the other.

For example, although not always recognized by both groups of employees, staff in both libraries and computing centers:

- develop training tools and system documentation;
- design and operate local area networks;
- plan and select system hardware and software;
- collect materials such as software;
- manage databases;
- perform systems analyses;
- provide technical assistance and consulting advice; and
- instruct faculty, students, and staff in
    - searching strategies;
    - database creation;
    - file management techniques; and
    - network access.

In these activities, their goals are essentially the same: helping users to make optimum use of hardware, software, and communications systems to manipulate information-as-thing or information-as-process.

Observable evidence prior to the study seemed to indicate that jobs in libraries and computing centers were becoming indistinguishable from each another. In fact, without directional signs or knowing the location of a terminal, it is often difficult to tell whether the end-user and the supporting information workers are located at home, in an office, a computer lab, a library, or a computing center.Yet at the same time, "library" jobs and "computing" jobs have been and still are traditionally classified in different job streams or job families, with different pay scales, responsibility levels, and, sometimes, benefits. For example, librarians might have faculty status and benefits, while computing specialists doing the same work might not.

A Study of the Information Job Family

Experts agree that in the early stages of automation, the nature of the work being done remained essentially the same, but that it was augmented by new equipment, methods, and procedures. In later stages, however, when interactive online systems came to be used, studies have found that job content alters, and new knowledge, skills, abilities, and responsibilities are introduced. This is now such a firmly established principle that it is supported by labor relations arbitrations decisions (Brown, 1989).

While a number of studies have been conducted on the changes in jobs caused by advances in technology, most, with the exception of Zuboff's (1988), have been done in automated, not "informated," times and environments. Most examine one organization or one group of employees; therefore, little in previous studies that focus on changes in jobs due to advances in technology, provided guidance for our exploratory project.

According to a survey of information systems professionals by the Center for the Study of Data Processing, it was the opinion of information systems (IS) vice presidents and directors that the central IS role is "shifting away from its traditional focus on applications development" (Hartog and Brower, 1991) and will focus more on systems integration, technology evaluation, and providing consulting support to end-users (p. 25). An analysis of technological impact on skill needs in the armed forces led Binkin (1988) to conclude "that software maintenance is a manpower-intensive task but, because of its complexity, workload requirements are extremely difficult to forecast, especially in a distributed processing environment" (pp. 213-214). Spenner's macro-analysis of studies resulted in his conclusion that "the effects of technological change on the skill requirements of work are set in a larger context of market forces, managerial prerogatives (in implementing technologies), and organizational cultures, all of which condition the effects of technological change" (pp. 132-133). Further, "The forces of managers, markets, and organizational cultures are sufficient to reverse the effects of a technology on skill upgrading or downgrading" (p. 132).

Many of the studies on the effects of technology on jobs have led to recommendations that management pay attention to human resource issues, particularly the need for training and retraining programs (Mowshowitz, 1990). No studies were found in the computing, management, or library literature that examined "informated" jobs from the perspective of reward systems such as classification and compensation systems. As Rosenbaum (1980) points out, "studies of the determinants of individuals' earnings usually concentrate on individual characteristics." It was not until the early 1980s that some work was done on the mediating effects of occupational structures, mostly in corporate settings. Not surprisingly, many of these studies found that organizational levels of jobs mediated the influence of personal attributes such as gender and education, on earnings (p. 1-2). Rosenbaum found that organizational level hierarchy is an important structure upon which salaries are based.

No studies were found that examined changes in jobs in information units in higher education from the point of view of job content and salaries. At present, libraries and computing centers are typically seen as two cultures, at least as represented in the published literature of both groups. Most colleges and universities treat the two groups as different job families in their classification and compensation structures.

This research project therefore set out to test the hypothesis that in campus settings that are at the "informated" stages in their use of the information technologies, jobs in libraries and computing centers in particular will have altered significantly enough to identify a single new job family out of two or more traditionally separate job families. A lesser, but nevertheless important objective of the study, since it was exploratory (heuristic), was to find a bench-mark methodology which could show, even in gross terms, whether the changing nature of library and computing jobs was resulting in the overlapping and blending of tasks and compensable factors.

For the study, the University of Pittsburgh permitted use of its recently developed point factor job analysis system. This enabled analysis of jobs on eleven factors (see Table 1) and assignment of points according to the degree to which a job possessed a particular factor. The strength of the system was that it not only allowed for identification of the most important compensable factors for each job, but its point system also approximated a coding structure for content analysis.

Knowledge
Experience
Degree of Supervision Received
Analytical Skills
Financial Responsibility
Impact of Actions
Nature of Supervision Received
Scope of Human Resources Impact
Internal Contacts
External Contacts
Physical Effort

Table 1. Job evaluation factors.

Three institutions were selected as sites for the study on the basis of the following criteria:

- Each had been deemed by peer judgement to be beyond automation and be at the "informated" stage in use of the information technologies;

- Each had a high degree of administrative integration potential with both the academic computing center and the library reporting to the same person;

- The library and the academic computing center had the potential to be at the same organizational level hierarchically, with both reporting to a CIO;

- Each was a relatively large academic institution; and, of course,

- Each agreed to participate.

Job descriptions from each participating library and academic computing center were collected and reviewed for completeness and recency. A data collection form was sent to each site to use in supplying information or job descriptions which were missing or out of date. Each description was cross-checked against organization charts to verify that all jobs and job levels were represented. The job descriptions were then encoded to ensure anonymity through the rest of the study. Duplicate job descriptions were eliminated. That is to say, if one description was the same for six reference librarians, one description, not six, was used in the study. To confine jobs in the study solely to those that did purely "library" and "computing" work, all administrative, secretarial, vacant, frozen, and part-time positions were eliminated from the valuative portion of the study. The result was that out of 371 descriptions, 63 unique jobs were identified for full analysis. To ensure that all types of jobs were represented, each site was asked to review the final selection for omissions. The researchers were confident that a complete snapshot of each sites' current library and computing jobs was available for the study.

As a final step, the descriptions were stripped of their overlay of library and computing jargon. And they were replete with professional vernacular! This step enabled the principal investigator to translate jargon-ridden sentences into language that all members of the evaluation teams could understand. A site visit took place during which the principal investigator worked with a team at each site to determine the points to be assigned for the eleven factors for each job.

Preliminary Findings

The analysis currently underway has yielded quantitative and qualitative assessments that will only be highlighted here.[2]

What was discovered was that many jobs are similar in part, a small number had no similarities, and another small number were identical. It is this last group that obviously proved most interesting to the study.

The following jobs were found in both libraries and computing centers:

1. Systems analysis and design, involving programming for microcomputer applications and micro-mainframe interfaces, network design, implementation and maintenance, and preparing system documentation and operations guides;

2. User services, involving preparation of end-user documentation, individual and group instruction in how to use online systems, applications software, networks, and peripherals such as CD-ROM and scanners;

3. Resource building, involving the acquisition of software and other information products for faculty, students and staff, and organizing and publicizing these files, materials, and services for users; and

4. Support services, such as data entry (on- and off-line); development and maintenance of databases, both for internal operating purposes (e.g. lists of "users" and profiles of their service needs, billing, etc.); generation and analysis of reports from transaction logs of systems operations to identify usage levels by type and category of users.

Pieces of jobs that were similar were more difficult to identify, mostly because tasks were described in technical or professional jargon instead of plain English. However, if acronyms and trademarks are removed from their job descriptions, it was difficult to find differences between a reference librarian's job and an academic computer-center end-user consultant's. To illustrate with a specific example from the academic library setting, the first sentence is typical of many job descriptions in libraries:

1. "Checks in standing orders on XXXX system . . . . Monitors problems and works on their resolution with OCLC."

Compare this with two sentences from computing center jobs:

2. "Designs, tests, maintains, and modifies computer-based information systems . . ."

3. "Operates data entry devices and performs all types of data entry . . ."

It is not easy to determine whether the first job is most similar to second or third. It is easy to imagine that a job analyst who is not familiar with libraryese could easily think that #1 is more similar to #3 than to #2. On site, a translation of the first job into real English, revealed that it was a position almost solely responsible for ensuring the accuracy and maintenance of a portion of the campus-wide database (OPAC, if you will). The title used for the position was "library assistant"—subtitled "serials acquisition assistant." Job #2 was a systems analyst position, and after discussion of the impact of actions and other factors, the serials acquisition assistant and the system analyst positions were assigned the same number of points. The data entry operator position represented in #3 was awarded fewer points than the other two jobs.

With very little effort, it is easy to relegate each of these jobs to traditional "library" or "computing center" activities on the basis of title alone. Perhaps if the serials acquisition assistant were called a "database manager" or some other more universally understood title, there would be less devaluation of it. If it were stripped of language only understood by librarians, the job might well exist in a computing center as easily as in a library. In short, not only do the tasks and positions exist in both worlds, but they can no longer be distinguished as belonging in one or the other. Yet, lack of clarity and uniform language form barriers that continue to divide our views and assumptions about the kind of work done in the two settings. And as a result, different assumptions are also made about appropriate levels of compensation.

The study also asked questions about the comparability of library and computing jobs on measures such as skills and qualifications. Here, too, the study has yielded some answers.

Analytical skills were found to be significant in both sets of jobs. The work in both organizations is very similar in complexity, scope, and breadth of the functional areas covered. Most positions in both settings deal with work that is nonstandardized and widely varied, involving many complex and significant variables. The mean of all jobs required a level of analytical ability and inductive thinking that can deal with extensive adaptation of policies, procedures, and methods to fit unusual or complex decisions. This was the level assigned, for example, to positions such as programmers and copy catalogers, if the "two cultures" want familiar examples.

Knowledge, as measured by educational level, was also found to be a significant factor in both library and computing jobs. The MLS as a basic professional degree was apparent in libraries, while there was no similar threshold identified for computing jobs. As a result, there was much more variety in the educational levels represented in computing centers.

Span of contacts, internal and external, to the university, was rated high for both sets of jobs, and especially so when related to analytical skills and knowledge. The impact of actions resulting from library and computing center activities also scored high. In fact, the jobs were valued for using knowledge and analysis for a broadly based university population (internal contacts), as well as involvement with contacts outside the university (external contacts); and the impact of these interactions are considered important.

Penrod, in an earlier chapter indicated that in the relationship of IT and the basic elements necessary to re-engineering, IT is seen as a basic tool to empower individual employees. In terms of the factors used in our study, this empowerment is probably most readily measured in terms of the amount of supervision received—or the degree of autonomy given to individuals to do their work. Both library and computing center jobs are done under "general direction, working from broad goals and policies only. Incumbents participate heavily in setting the work objectives." In all three organizations, the mean raw score of points assigned to library jobs was slightly (but not significantly) higher than for computing jobs.

In other words, a high degree of autonomy already appears to exist in jobs in computer centers and libraries—at least in the three organizations studied. On the assumption that autonomy in setting one's own objectives translates into that sexy new term, "empowerment," one of the elements needed to transform the IRM partners on campus is already embedded in both sets of jobs.

You are probably saying, "Of course! I know that." And we would agree that such job content similarities ought to appear to anyone even slightly familiar with computing and library environments. The study, however, has made the evidence more than anecdotal, and has suggested a methodology for reexamining job families which could be applied in many organizational settings.

The Missing Links

Studies are also interesting for what they discover missing. What was found lacking in the organizations studied were the following:

- Instructions are needed on how to write job descriptions that are comparable. This means developing glossaries that standardize technical terms such as "OPAC" and "LIUNET" into "campus-wide databases" and "wide-area networks." Tasks such as "check in" "copy cataloging," "take bug reports and user requests," and even general terms such as "assist" and "coordinate" need to be distinguished from one another by use of standardized definitions.

- There is also a critical need for rationalizing salary and benefit policies/systems between librarians and computing specialists. Among the jobs in the study, the total factor points were 23 percent higher for the library cohort of jobs, but salaries were 13 percent higher for the computing group. Considering that 42 percent of all salaries in the libraries were lower than the lowest computer center salary, this rationalization process takes on even greater significance.

- Also needed is a dialogue leading to closer coordination of objectives, function, and the work done by the various information partners on campus. Even on the relatively well-integrated campuses in this study, one computing center we visited was unaware the library had a CD-ROM LAN operating and that the library had the expertise to set it up and operate it. In yet another instance, the library and the computing center had agreed on a very clear division of responsibility for acquisition and organization of the institution's software and hardware.

The Chief Integration Officer

In two of the three settings, the job evaluation project brought together managerial-level library and computing center staff who obviously had not had much prior contact with one another. Impressionistic evidence is that neither of those two groups know much about the work of the other even though they coexist in the same organization under a CIO. This impression confirms evidence from an earlier study of CIOs and librarians in 1986-87: that library directors and CIOs, more often than not, did not have a closely matched perception of the degree of control that the CIO exercised over the library's information technologies (Woodsworth, 1988).

To come full circle, on the basis of the job study the presence of the CIO has not, as yet, ensured an integration of the infrastructure below the administrative level. While both the technologies and work are "integrating" the infrastructure is not. As one pundit expressed it, perhaps what we need is a Chief Integration Officer!

Earlier in this book Jane Ryland pictured an action plan to transform our academic institutions. She emphasized the need for incentives to achieve transformation through information management, as follows:

- for faculty: particularly through the tenure and promotion system;

- for students: through an entertainment factor in the learning experience; and

- for the administration: through better results for less effort and time expended.

A very important group was omitted in Ryland's description—the 75 percent who are the working center of our colleges and universities (all non-faculty personnel). This group also needs incentives. They need more than just training in the use of the information technologies and ease of use to make them more productive. For those who are key in introducing the information technologies and systems into the organizational infrastructure (those in computing, library, and telecommunications), a financial incentive such as recognition of their contribution through a rational reward structure will be necessary. Their need is for the organizational infrastructure to recognize and reward their work in an equitable way across the organization. They are, in many instances, already doing work that has been transformed. In the main, it is their work that has and will be redesigned. The diffusion of the kinds of work and tasks now being performed in libraries and computing centers will become more prevalent in all parts of the campus as computing (information-as-process) and information-as-thing (e.g. CD-ROMs, CWIS databases) are managed and used on a distributed model.

As Ryland pointed out (p. 6) financial incentives are a powerful motivation for "transformation." Not only will they drive organizations to rationalize operations, but this in turn will ultimately lead to forced rationalization of jobs and concomitant job classification and reward systems. A clear message needs to go to college and university administrators to tackle this problem before it becomes a crisis. California State University's Chancellor's office has already begun to address the problem and to try to develop benchmark job descriptions and definitions.

This study, which we consider to be an heuristic one, clearly indicates that, at almost all operating levels, comparable jobs (and some identical jobs) do exist in libraries and computing centers. Their comparability is, however, hampered by traditional job classification systems and jargon-filled job descriptions. This can make meaningful dialogue among libraries, computing centers, and compensation analysis departments frustrating at best, and impossible, at worst. Either the presence of a CIO is immaterial, or the human and social issues have not yet reached sufficient crisis proportions to get a CIO's attention.

Creating a new family of jobs will offer expanded opportunities, and not only for those of us doing the work. It will also allow for providing integrated information services of many kinds to the information users, who are, after all, our reason for doing what we do. Perhaps the kinds of transformation and re-engineering described in this book will create a different meaning for CIO. Not "Chief Information Officer." Not "Career Is Over," as suggested by *Computerworld*. Transformation may cause it to mean "Changing Information Organizations" or "Change Is On-going." More radical yet, perhaps the next evolution in management acronyms that deal with the information technologies will be CIN—"Coordinator of Information Networks," or better yet, SIN—"Synergistic Integrated Networkers."

Notes

1. The Council on Library Resources provided funding for a study entitled "The Information Job Family: An Examination of the Effects of the Integrating Information Technologies on Job Classification and Compensation System" beginning January 1991 and originally ending December 1991. Due to the principal investigator's relocation, the end of the grant period was extended to April 30, 1992.

2. Apart from a final report to the Council on Library Resources, an article about the study appeared in *Library Trends*, volume 40, number 4 in 1992. Publication of the full report by CAUSE is also under discussion.

References

Bignell, L. (May 1989). "What Happened to Middle Management?" *Manage*, 29-30.

Binkin, M. (1988). "Technology and Skills: Lessons from the Military," In Cyert, R. M. and Mowery, D. C. (Eds.) *The Impact of Technological Change on Employment and Economic Growth*, 185-222. Cambridge, MA: Ballinger Publishing.

Brown, S. R. (1989). "New Technology: How Does It Affect the Workplace?" *The Arbitration Journal*, 44(3): 32-41.

Brumm, E. K. (1989). "Chief Information Officers in Service and Industrial Organizations," Paper presented at the American Society for Information Science Conference, Washington, DC, November 1, 1989.

Buckland, M. (1991). *Information and Information Systems*. New York: Praeger.

Byrne, J. A. (1988, September 12). "Caught in the Middle: Six Managers Speak Out on Corporate Life," *Business Week*, 80-88.

Drucker, P. F. (1988, April 18). "New Roles—New Rules: Tomorrow's Restless Managers," *Industry Week*, 25-27.

Fleit, L. H. "Choosing A Chief Information Officer: The Myth of The Computer Czar," *CAUSE/EFFECT*, 9 (3): 26-30.

Hartog, C. and Brower, R. (1991). *The New IS Professional: Prospects For The '90s*. Working Paper Series, vol. 4, no 1. St. Louis, MO: Center for the Study of Data Processing, Washington University.

McCredie, J. W. (Ed.). (1983). *Campus Computing Strategies*. Bedford, MA: Digital Press.

Micossi, A. (1990). "Work Design: The Quiet Revolution," *Enterprise*, 4 (1): 33-17.

Mowshowitz, A. (1990). "On Managing Technological Change," *Technovation*, 9: 623-633.

Penrod, J. I. (1992, March 5). "Transformation and the Chief Information Officer." Presentation at Computers in Libraries Conference, Washington, D.C.

Penrod, J. I., Dolence, M. G., and Douglas, J. V. (1990). *The Chief Information Officer in Higher Education*. Boulder, CO: CAUSE. Professional Paper # 4.

Potsdam College [advertisement]. (1991, February 20). *Chronicle of Higher Education*, p. B64.

Rosenbaum, J. E. (1980). "Hierarchical and Individual Effects on Earnings," *Industrial Relations*, *19* (1): 1-14.

Spenner, K. I. (1988). "Technological Change, Skill Requirements, and Education," In Cyert, R. M. and Mowery, D. C. (Eds.) *The Impact of Technological Change on Employment and Economic Growth*, 131-183. Cambridge, MA: Ballinger Publishing.

Synnott, W. R. and Gruber, W. H. (1981). *Information Resource Management: Opportunities and Strategies for the 1980s*. New York: John Wiley & Sons.

Wilder, C. (1992, February 17). "No Room at the Top: When the CIO Becomes Expendable," *Computerworld*, 1, 16.

Woodsworth, A. (1988). "Libraries and the Chief Information Officer: Implications and Trends," *Library Hi Tech*, *6* (1): 37- 44.

Woodsworth, A. (1991). *Patterns and Options for Managing Information Technology on Campus*. Chicago: American Library Association.

The Impact on the Academic Library: Political Issues

Joanne R. Euster

Introduction

From one point of view, all organizational planning and decision-making is political. This is particularly true where large-scale reallocations of resources are involved, where responsibilities (and hence territory and power) may be moved from one organizational unit to another, and where the long-term implications of policy decisions will affect numerous other segments of the institution.

This chapter describes the constituencies and stakeholders with which the library must negotiate or otherwise take into consideration as it plans, alone or in concert with other parts of the institution, for library and information services in a technological environment.

Stakeholders include the library's own current employees, formal and informal groups or coalitions of faculty, senior university administrators, and existing units with overlapping or competing spheres of responsibility, most notably computer centers and telecommunications services.

The success of the library in advancing its information agenda will depend on the extent to which it deals with issues of leadership, territory, control vs. empowerment, competition vs. collaboration, centralization and decentralization, and security vs. access, to name but a few of the more significant.

Favorable outcomes—those that support the library's mission and the institution's mission and goals—will depend on the institutions's ability to mobilize the abilities of the various power bases to work together across organizational boundaries in "instant coalitions" for the good of the entire institution. To do so requires skill in navigating around a complex set of belief systems involving conflicting organizational and professional cultures, historical precedents, and the fear of change.

Power and Politics

The great question which, in all ages, has disturbed mankind, and brought on them the greatest part of their mischiefs . . . has been, not

whether be power in the world, nor whence it came, but who should have it.
—John Locke, *An Essay Concerning Human Understanding*, 1690.

Knowledge itself is power.
—Francis Bacon, "Of Heresies," *Religious Meditations,* 1597.

politics (pol'i tiks) n. . . . use of intrigue or strategy in obtaining any position of power or control, as in business, university, etc. . . ."
The Random House Dictionary of the English Language,
second edition unabridged, 1987.

How does the computerization of the library and of organized information figure into the political processes on campuses? Politics, by definition, is a complex and often intangible art. To understand the political aspect, it may be useful to first consider the *formal* channels through which the library and information management functions might participate in campus planning.

The literature regarding the management and planning of entire campuses is astonishingly unconcerned with *either* libraries or computing. For example, in Barbara Scott's 1983 book, *Crisis Management in American Higher Education* (a *most* tantalizing title! Where better to find crises to manage than in information services?), one finds sections on philanthropy, state and other education commissions and other agencies, faculty, affirmative action, transformation of the curriculum, and the limitations of students. "Librarians, Suppliers, and Technologists" get two paragraphs (p. 97-98) listing ALA, AAP, AECT, ETS, CB as a "cluster of interest groups." Also coming in for knocks is the "cozy alliance between the book publishing industry and the new field of educational technology." Period. No mentions of libraries, computing, or knowledge industry in the index.

A more recent "bible" of higher education management, Thomas Tellefsen's *Improving College Management: An Integrated Systems Approach*, published in 1990, lists 79 "Decision Matrices"—everything from "Presidential Search and Selection" to "Faculty Performance Evaluation," "Central Stores Operation," and finally "Campus Parking Operations," but NO library services, and NO computing services. Each of the matrices enumerates the "participants in the decision-making process." The librarian is listed as a participant in the change in enrollment status of students where withdrawal from the institution is involved (p. 180). Page 125 also calls for an annual evaluation of library operations and adequacy of library holdings leading to an annual written report and recommendation for the library's acquisitions program; this is allotted one paragraph. Computing/data processing gets two pages (pp. 367-9) dealing exclusively with data processing for administrative records.

The good news is, I believe, that although these books are aimed at upper executives in academia, most do not actually *read* these manuals.

While the role of the library seems to get short shrift in treatises on institutional planning and management, in fact, many of us are in situations where library and information needs are taking a prominent position in college and university planning. Our own literature is full of case studies and planning models.

Furthermore, the high costs of large-scale library systems has not escaped scrutiny. The National Association of College and University Business Officers (NACUBO) in 1986 published a study of the automation of four large university libraries, and concluded that the planning processes were erratic at best, while their costs were high, and that "some form of cost-benefit analysis of automated systems is not only desirable, but necessary" (page 14). Although the case studies do not present the libraries in a particularly favorable light, the book cannot have failed to raise the awareness of financial officers of the desirability of automating.

EDUCOM, the association most identified with academic computing, has taken a leading role in publications, and in particular with books, concerned with the planning for computing in higher education. As early as 1975, EDUCOM published *Who Runs the Computer, Strategies for the Management of Computers in Higher Education*, followed by *Planning for Computing in Higher Education* in 1980, and then a series of planning compilations, the most germane to our discussion being *Organizing and Managing Information Resources on Campus*, by Brian Hawkins, in 1989, and *Campus Strategies for Libraries and Electronic Information*, edited by Caroline Arms, in 1990.

In *Who Runs the Computer?*, the earliest (1975) of the EDUCOM publications mentioned above, four stages of computing development are described. At the lowest level, the Initial Stage, there is little use, knowledge, understanding of computing, and little belief in its value. This is followed by the Basic Stage, during which some perception of the value and potential impact of computing has developed and there is some use of computing, although it may be via resources outside the institution. The third stage is called the Operational Stage, in which the value of many applications is recognized, internal expertise has developed, and one or more "computing centers" have been established. The final, or Extended Stage, involves widespread understanding of the applicability of computing to almost all operations at the institution, student and faculty use and knowledge are extensive, and although there is extensive central support, users participate in decision-making and decentralized operations are the rule.

Seventeen years later in the growth of computational power, astronomical improvements in price/performance, the development of client/server architecture, and service models, one cannot help being a little in awe of such early ability to describe a durable model of future growth. At the same time, it is forgivable, I believe, to interject some intermediate stages, or to extend and refine the final stage. The present state for most institutions, it appears, is beyond the Operational Stage, but many are not yet truly at the Extended Stage; let us assume Stage 3.5 as the present mode.

Although the 1975 volume made little if any reference to libraries specifically, by 1980 *Planning for Computing in Higher Education* included no fewer than five chapters on library automation by librarians, including one by Allen Veaner, "The Politics of Planning for Library Computing" (pp. 109-115). Veaner's observations, although focused on large-scale library system development exclusively, remain valid today. He describes three important political factors: the librarian's ability to persuade superior institutional officers that the program is essential; the degree to which the institution wants to maintain equity with peer institutions; and the librarian's ability to work with a variety of local constituencies, particularly in terms of their initial assumptions.

By 1989, Hawkins' *Organizing and Managing Information Resources on Campus* represented a new generation of planning treatises in that library functions were well integrated into the discussion, although probably not to the degree that librarians would hope. Arms' 1990 *Campus Strategies for Libraries and Electronic Information* is less a planning guide than a series of descriptions of library automation plans and activities at ten universities, OCLC, and RLG.

Knowledge, Assumptions, and Fears

Individual faculty, computing staff, and administrators—even librarians— come to the table with highly variable knowledge and experience. In one week I had two conversations: the first was with the vice president for academic affairs at one of the country's larger universities, in which he informed me that when all was said and done, the principal business of the library was to acquire and make accessible books and journals. "Not exactly . . ." I replied. The second was with the chair of the campus planning committee for a smaller liberal arts college seeking advice on library expansion plans. "I can't see the need for all this space; it's all going to be on computers anyway, isn't it?" "Not exactly . . ." I explained, once again.

The present state of affairs is rather complex, and could be thought of as a matrix of awareness and knowledge of a highly changeable field. Those involved with planning include librarians, computing professionals, other academic administrators and faculty, and top academic officers—

presidents, and vice presidents. Understanding of information resources can be seen as a continuum from the most traditional of library functions (think in terms of a hypothetical college library before 1950), to the most visionary electronic, fully networked information service, with every conceivable permutation in between. Even among librarians there is wide variation in such essentials as comprehension of the extent of need, the complexities and interdependencies that must be considered, as well as ability to articulate with institutional realities such as how to get from here to there, balancing desirable functions against costs, and finally the need to build in future flexibility, expandability, and adaptability.

The library's role is as planner, but also as explainer, informer, educator, and interpreter. It is clearly not universally self-evident that the library's role as stakeholder in planning and managing information resources is broader than automating the manual processes associated with the print-centered library. Why? When the nature of information changes, when the nature of the delivery mechanisms changes, and above all, when the *concept* of information changes, a host of uncertainties is created, giving rise in turn to all the fears inherent in change—of threats to control, to territory, and to self-image. Few, indeed, are going to voluntarily turn over the management of change to another office, unless that agency has an outstanding track record of building trust and credibility, and perhaps not even then.

In the era of automating back-office library operations—cataloging, circulation, serials control, acquisitions—and development of the online public catalog as a computerized version of the card catalog, the library's task was essentially to persuade upper administration that the service improvements were worth the costs involved. For most large libraries there was little contention for the territory itself: the automation effort was computerization of the library alone, and even if the project was assisted or even operated by central computing services, the "ownership" of it remained with the library.

Now, however, the agenda has been elevated substantially, to go beyond meta-information, i.e., information about information, and aspires now first to meta-information from literally anywhere in the world and about any format or publishing medium, and second to the actual information itself. The information world has become one of networks, listservers, scholarly exchange of information, publication of both organized and unorganized information, imaging, facsimile transmission, remote access to information and information about information. In recognition of this world, a growing number of institutions is acknowledging and addressing the need for students to become information literate, not as a tool for getting through their academic careers, but as an essential skill for living and working.

Unquestionably, not all of this territory falls to the library. Nor, to my mind, does it fall to *any* single organizational unit. The boundaries between stakeholders have become blurred, and an entire new class of stakeholders has emerged: the faculty and students, which is to say, the clients, customers, and users. To be sure, "library automation" was designed to serve them better, but the technology was an intermediate means, not a direct user service. The turning point came with the introduction of the OPAC, which had hardly been turned on before faculty were asking how to access it from their home computers, and students were complaining that journal articles were not included.

With ill-defined territories—and it should be understood that fuzzy definition is less a matter of poor organization than it is an artifact of technological complexity and continuous change—new models of planning and decision-making, and perhaps even of operations, are required. The present paradigm, however, continues to be the assignment and delegation of responsibility and authority as represented in the traditional organization chart. Not only does the present segmented bureaucratic design of academic institutions run counter to the cross-cutting functionality of computing, but both the compartmentalization of the organization and the academic culture tend to militate against rapid planning, decision-making and implementation. As the half-life of technologies continues to decline, the temporal frame may be the single most limiting factor colleges and universities face!

Librarians and academics are comfortable with such constructs as user groups, cooperative endeavors, and advisory committees. Are these adequate to the task? Perhaps, but they have the weakness of being appended to an organizational *modus operandi* which focuses first on boundaries and territories, and only secondarily on integration. Ideally, one might posit an organizational construct so fluid and flexible that it would be permeable at any point. Pragmatically, the need is for models that extend but do not exceed the limits of our ability to conceptualize.

The coalition model offers considerable potential. Coalitions can pool their resources to accomplish a given objective. Yet because they have identities of their own, but are "owned" by their principals, they do not threaten existing territories. The instant coalition may well become the planning and implementation instrument of choice. Regardless, the imperative is for what might be characterized as open collaboration or an internal partnership rather than simple negotiation and division of territory. Under even the most optimistic scenario, extraordinary political skills will be required, and those who exercise those skills earliest and with greatest tact are likely to emerge as leaders.

Diverse parties come to the partnership table to form a coalition based on interest, need, expertise, and previously defined responsibilities. They bring desires for power and for control, or fear of loss of what power they now have. They fear win-lose situations. The skillful librarian politician will understand the expectations, fears, and values the stakeholders bring with them and will work toward win-win situations. Throughout, the key question will be how to actually work together over time, via subdivision of work into meaningful units that continues to maintain coherence in the organizational context.

The Coalition Stakeholders

The primary stakeholders impacting the library and its use of computing/ telecommunications resources in meeting its goals include senior university administrators, students, faculty, the library's professional and managerial staff, its support staff, and campus organizational units with overlapping or competing spheres of responsibility and expertise, most notably, computer centers and telecommunications services. Faculty and graduate students represent such diverse knowledge and expectations that it is necessary to further subdivide them according to disciplinary needs, according to academic structure on a campus. Science faculty who have extensive experience with computing will have different perspectives from social scientists, who in turn differ from humanists, while professional school faculty will bring yet further idiosyncracies to the mix.

Library Assumptions and Values

It would be folly to assume that the values held by librarians are sacrosanct, and hence above examination. In the permeable environment of coalitions, everything must be open to discussion and negotiation. Let us turn first, then, to the stakeholder group we know the best.

Librarians have a longstanding pattern, reinforced by presidents and others who make periodic statements of fealty to libraries as the heart of the university or college, of assuming that the library's definition of value is that of the entire institution—or would be, if only administrators and faculty could be led to see the light. When—if ever—the library was able to stand somewhat aloof from the institution, in the world where we too often spoke of "the library" and "the university" as if they were distinct and only loosely connected entities, it was easier to maintain this comfortably pious belief. In the electronic environment of continuous and rapid change, with nearly every step dependent on collaboration with a variety of constituencies and stakeholders, it is not possible to promulgate certain values, however widely they may be accepted in the final analysis, and expect them to go unchallenged or to be accepted *prima facie*.

There are three library values that are most likely to come into question: (1) the library's service orientation vs. the customer orientation of an information agency, (2) the extent to which information is free to users, and, (3) cost effectiveness as a criterion in allocation of resources. Debate on these issues will inevitably occur.

Service Orientation vs. Customer Orientation. The Total Quality Management (TQM) movement makes much of the notion that the purpose of every organization and every worker within the organization is to serve its customers, to give customers what *they* want. The professional orientation, however, assumes that the expertise *and knowledge of what is good, useful, or valuable to the client* resides with the professional and the organization, and in what we might call the medical model, the mission is to serve the client by prescribing services or products. Alternatively, the—let us say— Levi Strauss model produces what the customer wants and is willing to pay for, either in cash or in time and effort to acquire the goods or service. The goal of the organization is to satisfy the customer, and every decision and action should be capable of justification in terms of customer satisfaction.

Academic libraries clearly belong in the first category; special and corporate libraries and information services have tended toward the latter. As a field, librarians have preferred the medical service model as a matter of professional status and pride. Examination of the issue in the context of our total institutional goals and the multiple competing needs of various constituencies may lead us, however, to shift our orientation to another point on the continuum between the two extremes.

Free Information. As a profession, librarians have not yet truly engaged the issue of charging for information. We know there is no such thing as "free" information, any more than clean water or air are truly free. The question is rather, Who pays? Furthermore, academic libraries studiously avoid recognizing the costs in time and inconvenience we regularly impose on users. In addition, we confuse cost and price, even in our own minds. Finally, we often fail to acknowledge that there can be multiple purposes in charging for information beyond simple cost recovery, and in so doing deny ourselves the option of using pricing as a method of allocating a scarce resource among competing customers. Interaction and collaboration with agencies—computing and telecommunications—that have routinely charged for services and have the capability to use a variety of modes for accounting and charging will inevitably place libraries in the position of reexamining the role of charges for value added, expensive, or esoteric (by whatever definition) services.

Cost Effectiveness as a Resource Allocation Criterion. Collectively, we are poor at determining what our activities cost, in part because we are equally poor at deciding what is a measurable output. Items circulated? Items processed? Questions answered? How well? We count what is easily counted, without regard for whether it tells us anything about how we are using resources, or how we *should* allocate resources. Regardless of how strongly one supports bibliographic instruction, our assessments of its value are highly subjective. We are at a loss as to how to come to grips with such issues as whether brief introductory bibliographic instruction session via a videotape for all students is better/worse/no different vs. face-to-face instruction by a librarian in course-related instruction. Arguing that the comparison is apples and oranges does not answer the question, How can the library best use its limited resources?

The belief, implicit or explicit, that the library is a *prima facie* "good" has led librarians to ignore cost/benefit analyses. The reasoning seems to go something like this: If the library is of unquestioned and limitless value to the institution, then it should and will receive all the funds the institution can be persuaded to invest in it; put another way, if the library is an institutional priority, "adequate" (read "more") financial resources will be found.

This assumption verges dangerously close to the "printing press" model of allocation of funds. In fact, *every* allocation decision means that money will not be spent on something else; even "new" money expended on the library means that some other potential new use is foregone. In addition, greater public pressures for cost containment—witness the furor over indirect cost rates for funded research, or student protests over even small tuition increases, or the continuing press attention to the growth in the costs of higher education, particularly if extended out until your newborn child enters college—are bringing all areas of the institution under closer scrutiny for clear justifications of expenditures. Libraries and computing centers are increasingly seen as black holes capable of absorbing infinite resources, and so far as having failed to realize the promise of technology and collaboration to improve services *and* reduce costs.

Having looked at our own house, we are perhaps in a better position to anticipate the assumptions and concerns other parties bring to the coalition. Each individual brings certain human needs: the desire to have control over one's own work life, the desire to know the full scope of the activity and how it fits into the larger scheme, and the desire to feel valued and proud of his or her contributions. In addition, the library's customers want to feel valued and enjoy some reasonable level of comfort that the library will reliably have the resources they need readily available. The savvy politician will remember that whatever positions are promulgated, or however worthy the organizational goals offered, these individual desires will also come into play. Now let us turn to the principal external stakeholders.

Faculty as Stakeholders

Faculty, although they may be represented by a single group, such as a Senate committee, in fact have widely—even wildly—divergent needs, expectations, and expertise where computing is involved, and many would say the same of their relationship to libraries. The three volumes produced by the Research Libraries Group on research needs of scholars in the humanities, social sciences, and sciences give an excellent picture of how various faculties conduct their research, and how they approach their information needs. Their understanding of what either libraries or computers can do in practical and organizational terms is particularized and idiosyncratic, at best. In the past two years many libraries have presented symposia and seminars on various aspects of scholarly communication in an effort to build a common knowledge base and language of discourse about information technology among faculty. Although strong leadership is critical, the development of this populist knowledge base is equally important for faculty, and as I will point out later, for administrators.

Many faculty in the humanities and social sciences feel overwhelmed and neglected by their science colleagues, whose claims to intensive computing cycles and greater knowledge of the technology somehow seem to position them not only as principal users of information technology, but as principal decision makers as well. In a "Point of View" column in *The Chronicle of Higher Education* in 1991, Douglas Greenberg, vice president of the American Council of Learned Societies, articulated this difficulty on behalf of humanists, claiming, "The results of the new technology, in other words, may be democratic in substance, but they are elitist with respect to access . . . . The real problem, at least in the humanities, is not excess but access."

Students

Undergraduate students will be concerned with universality of access and with support for course-related work. They may or may not see the potential for computing throughout teaching and learning, but inevitably their primary agenda will be to meet their immediate short-term needs. Graduate students' concerns are likely to bridge those of undergraduates and the faculty in their disciplines.

Computing Services

At the Information Services retreat held at Rutgers University in May 1991, computing professionals described themselves, in discussions with librarians, as being more oriented to machines than people, to product rather than process, to individual rather than group work, and to rapid decision-making rather than evolutionary processes. These are important basic behavior patterns, founded in assumptions about how organizations function and how work gets done. Coalitions will need to come to, if not agreement, at least detente about operating styles. Rapidly changing technology argues for prompt decision-making and implementation, a style that in general is not the hallmark of higher education, nor of librarianship.

There has been extensive discussion in academic computing literature and at conferences about the value of the library's service orientation, and its extension to computing services. The extent to which libraries and computing share this value is uncertain, although it is undoubtedly growing. Information technology as a populist tool is still too new for one to safely assume that its somewhat elitist origins have not left their mark. Librarians tend to work in groups, hold frequent meetings, and resolve issues by consensus and only after extensive discussion. Computing professionals, by their own description, see teamwork as a matter of coordination, find meetings to be diversions from "real work," and to rely on their technical skill in preference to user advice.

Academic Administrators

Campus administrators, regardless of their hierarchical relationship to the library, bear the additional burden of responsibility for the overall balance of allocation of campus resources, and for the ultimate educational and research quality of the institution. While assumptions of intrinsic value have always been questioned at this level, in difficult economic times even greater scrutiny is applied to resource allocation decisions. New programs and activities are regarded with skepticism, particularly if they do not replace *and* perform more effectively an existing activity or service. At the same time, there has been—and still persists in many institutions—the assumption that problems can be easily and cheaply resolved by technology, without the concomitant understanding of the myriad complexities and the continuing costs of most technological "fixes."

Thus it is vital that the library not only promote new information resources and services, but that the library be continuously engaged in educating senior campus administration about the range and capabilities of technology for improving access to information and the breadth of the information resources that can be made available. If this sort of groundwork is laid, selling particular projects will be much easier—not necessarily *easy*, but *easier*. Of course, the more knowledgeable the campus administration, the more thorough their review is likely to be.

Each library will have its own set of strategies for building campus administrative knowledge and support. A sample of strategies that campuses have found successful:

- A regular and frequent flow of short articles, clippings, newsletters, and abstracts that focus on building an administrative knowledge base; *Library Issues*, a bimonthly newsletter published by Mountainside Publishing, is aimed at a faculty and administrative audience, and many libraries distribute it amongst academic administrators.

- Campus-wide seminars on aspects of the scholarly information process; aimed at both faculty and administrators, these have recently become popular. They are usually designed to increase understanding and to involve the entire campus in the national debate over the future of scholarly information.

- Nothing succeeds like success: implementation of successful small projects that benefit users, including administrators, is a powerful way to demonstrate the likelihood of success in larger (and more costly) projects.

The emphasis on costs and accountability, of course, leads to the requirement for ever more thorough planning, cost analysis, and justification of proposals. At the same time, the wise librarian will remember that while busy administrators want adequate detail, they also expect to be able to understand the scope of a proposal quickly; accordingly, executive summaries of no more than two pages should arrive as the cover for all documentation.

A good plan will include, at minimum:

- The objectives of the project; what it will accomplish.

- Why is it appropriate to do it now? How rapidly is the technology or state of the art changing, and what are the best estimates of the state three to five years from now? What implications does this have for future costs?

- What are the costs, initial and ongoing? What are the alternatives for phasing funding over multiple years; if there are cost savings, what is the payback period, and how is it calculated?

- Are additional staff required? Alternatively, will staff reductions or redeployment be possible?

- What alternatives exist? Continue the present operation; implement only a portion of the project; in-house development versus purchase?

- What are the implications for improved services to faculty and students? How do you know users want or will take advantage of the service? Is there "value added" implicit in the proposal? Will the proposal in any way add to the institution's competitive advantage in recruiting and retaining students and faculty?

- How does this plan position your institution vis-a-vis its peer group of institutions?

Library Employees as Stakeholders

Not to be forgotten, at least within the library, are the considerably less than monolithic groups of library employees: librarians, administrators, supervisory and technical personnel, and support staff. In the early days of computing, support staff were torn between two conflicting sets of emotions: the excitement and fear of learning a new technology, and worries about how introduction of a new technology might add to their workload *or* eliminate their jobs altogether. Two decades of library automation experience have lessened the fears to some extent. However, staff are well aware of the cost-cutting pressures on higher education, and it would be foolish to assume that job security concerns have disappeared. In addition, increased sophistication has introduced two further issues. Use of a more advanced technology may result in job or classification upgrades; whether it does or not, the expectation will be present, and should be dealt with early. The second issue has to do with training. Beyond the desire to be well equipped to do their jobs well, most staff are eager to develop computer skills which they see as important for personal development as well as for their work.

Supervisors and middle managers will reflect staff concerns; time spent in advance planning for change, training, consulting and communicating plans will be well spent, *even if many details are changed later after there is experience with the system.* The two greatest pitfalls for managerial and technical staff are disregarding the operational staff's need to know (RULE: Staff always want to know more than management thinks they need to know!), and making global assumptions about the capabilities of a new system and its ability to solve current problems.

The Library Leadership Role

The library needs to take an aggressively proactive role in establishing the coalitions surrounding computerization of the campus. Its leadership role derives from two strengths: first, the extensive experience and success of libraries over the last hundred years or more in organizing and designing methods of access to recorded information resources, which is well recognized in academia. Secondly, there is the expertise librarians have in managing processes among individuals and groups. Librarians are often faulted for paying excessive attention to process in planning and decision-making; in the world of instant or enduring coalitions, this is a rare and valuable skill, the more significant since an important group of players, computing professionals, tends to be more oriented to product than to process.

The library's information agenda will be promulgated and defended by its director; however, in the final analysis, its success will be heavily dependent on the extent to which the library *as a whole* has been successful in its leadership on the campus.

References

Arms, Caroline, ed., *Campus Strategies for Libraries and Electronic Information.* (EDUCOM Strategies Series on Information Technology) Digital Press, 1990.

Emery, James C. ed., *Planning for Computing in Higher Education.* (EDUCOM Series in Computing and Telecommunications in Higher Education; 5) Boulder, CO: Westview Press, 1980.

Gould, Constance C. *Information Needs in the Humanities: An Assessment.* Stanford, CA: Research Libraries Group, 1988.

Gould, Constance C. *Information Needs in the Social Sciences: An Assessment.* Mountain View, CA: Research Libraries Group, 1989.

Gould, Constance C. *Information Needs in the Sciences: An Assessment.* Mountain View, CA: Research Libraries Group, 1991.

Greenberg, Douglas, "Information Access: Our Elitist System Must be Reformed." *The Chronicle of Higher Education,* volume XXXVIII, number 9, October 23, 1991, A48.

Hawkins, Brian L., ed., *Organizing and Managing Information Resources on Campus.* (EDUCOM Strategy Series on Information Technology) McKinney, Texas: Academic Computing Publications, 1989.

Hyatt, James A., *University Libraries in Transition.* Washington, DC: National Association of College and University Business Officers, 1986.

Robbins, Martin D., William S. Dorn, and John E. Skelton *Who Runs the Computer? Strategies for the Management of Computers in Higher Education.* Boulder, CO: Westview Press, 1975.

Scott, Barbara Ann. *Crisis Management in American Higher Education.* New York: Praeger, 1983.

Tellefsen, Thomas E. *Improving College Management: An Integrated Systems Approach,* San Francisco: Jossey-Bass, 1990.

Management Issues in the "Informated" Library

Charles B. Lowry

Introduction

The public discussion of how the new paradigm of the "virtual" library will develop, and what roles it will play in the delivery of information, point to the many problems which will have to be resolved, but usually describe a bright future. This vision of the future depicts an information-rich environment, what that will mean to library users, and how information technology will mediate this environment. It also elaborates on the politics of change and what library managers must do to insure effective participation in this process, particularly organizational change and resource allocation.

This is an exciting and fruitful dialogue at professional meetings, in journals, and on the electronic text called Internet. It reflects and in turn stimulates the transformation which information technology is "driving," but the discussion concentrates more on the external effects on library users and the institutional environment in which libraries exist. It is of equal importance to consider that this change is doing something inside libraries—to organization and to staff—something which is "transformational" to a significant degree. Zuboff has studied this process in which information technology "informates" an organization, and the research in library organization presented in this chapter reflects many of her findings. In libraries the informating process is advancing through the wholesale application of information technology, especially the applications of integrated systems, local area networks (LANs) applied to management purposes, and broad participation by library employees in "cutting-edge" changes caused by the medium of the Internet/BITNET.

Paradigm Shift—Limits of Thinking

Discussion in the professional literature of librarianship has emphasized the need to shift to a new paradigm for academic and research libraries.[1] The concept of paradigms developed by T. S. Kuhn is, after all, a powerful tool for thinking in both sciences and social sciences. "The paradigm is something which can function when the theory is not there . . . [and which] . . . has got to be a concrete picture used analogically; because it has got to be a way of seeing."[2] Charles Martell summarized the extent of this discussion succinctly.

"The warehouse, or collection-based paradigm still holds sway. The center-piece of this paradigm is the provision of items shelved locally. A new access-based paradigm is emerging and gaining many adherents. Its centerpiece is the provision of items wherever they may be located. What happens between the user and the content of items is beyond the boundary of either paradigm."[3]

Perhaps the most visionary example of thinking about the paradigm shift for libraries was recently offered by Marvin Minsky of MIT in Ray Kurzweil's book *The Age of Intelligent Machines*. Minsky's future library is to some extent a latter-day version of Vannevar Bush's Memex.

> The libraries of today are warehouses for passive objects. The books and journals sit on shelves waiting for us to use our intelligence to find them, read them, interpret them, and cause them finally to divulge their stored knowledge. Electronic libraries of today are no better. Their pages are pages of data files, but the electronic pages are equally passive.

> Now imagine the library as an active, intelligent knowledge server. It stores the knowledge of the disciplines in complex knowledge structures (perhaps in a knowledge-representation formalism yet to be invented). It can reason with this knowledge to satisfy the needs of its users. These needs are expressed naturally, with fluid discourse. The system can, of course, retrieve and exhibit (i.e., it can act as an electronic textbook). It can collect relevant information; it can summarize; it can pursue relationships. It acts as a consultant on specific problems, offering advice on particular solutions, justifying those solutions with citations or with a fabric of general reasoning. . . . The user of the library of the future need not be a person. It may be another knowledge system, that is, any intelligent agent with a need for knowledge. Thus, the library of the future will be a network of knowledge systems in which people and machines collaborate. Publishing will be an activity transformed. Authors may bypass text, adding their increment to human knowledge directly to the knowledge structures. Since the thread of responsibility must be maintained, and since there may be disagreement as knowledge grows, the contributions are authored (incidentally allowing for the computation of royalties for access and use). Maintaining the knowledge base (updating knowledge) becomes a vigorous part of the new publishing industry.[4]

As far as they go, the current discussions of the new library paradigm have dealt with only one dimension of the change required of libraries, and have not done full justice to Kuhn's concept. The discussion concentrates more on the external effects on library users and the institutional environment in which libraries exist. This emerging paradigm of the "virtual" library indeed is credible. However, it is past time to proceed further with its development and to give consideration to the effects of this change as the so-called "virtual" or "electronic library" becomes a reality. It is of equal importance to consider that this change is doing something inside libraries—to organization and to staff—something which is transformational to a significant degree. The central feature of this new library is a comprehensive use of computers and related information technologies. How will this affect library organization, human resources, and the need for professional education and training? Peter Drucker proposed the issues quite succinctly when he said that it is "right to ask if we are redefining libraries' mission. No, we are not redefining their mission, but we are redefining resources and as a result the role of librarians is changing."[5]

"Informated" Organizations

To understand what is just beginning to happen in libraries, we need only look at what happened in other organizations when whole processes were automated. In the industrial setting, the introduction of a high degree of automation based on information technology has transformed the nature of work, but the products remain the same. Cars are still cars and televisions are still televisions, even when CAD/CAM is used to design and build them. Banking services are highly automated and international, but they are still banking services. What has changed is the life of the workers in these new environments. That will happen for knowledge workers in libraries, as well. But there is an added dimension of complexity for libraries which is not present in the "knowledge-based" private sector. As Drucker's comment implies, their product, what we might call the knowledge format, is also changing. One must assume that this level of abstraction and complexity in which the tools of information technology also become the product distributed to library users will profoundly affect library organizations and librarianship as a profession.

With her groundbreaking book *In the Age of the Smart Machine: The Future of Work and Power*, Shoshana Zuboff introduced the idea that automation in modern industry and business is causing a revolution as dramatic as that caused by the mechanization of workshops and factories in Britain between 1789 and 1848 at the dawn of the industrial age. In a ten-year study of applied automation, she analyzed these fundamental changes, and the insights are directly applicable in the library setting.

On the one hand, technology can be applied to automating operations according to a logic that hardly differs from that of the 19th-
century machine system. . . . On the other, the same technology
simultaneously generates information about the underlying productive and administrative processes through which an organization accomplishes its work. It provides a deeper level of transparency to activities that had been either partially or completely
opaque. In this way, information technology supersedes the traditional logic of automation. The word that I have coined to describe this unique capacity is *informate*. Activities, events, and
objects are translated into and made visible by information when
a technology *informates* as well as *automates*.[6]

This conclusion has been broadly acclaimed as an original insight.
How it will apply to libraries is the question at hand.

While automation has often been associated with a general decline
in the degree of know-how and a routinization of the role of the individual
worker, there is plenty of evidence to indicate that automation also may have
extremely positive effects organizationally. In the first place, the broad application of information technologies can demand a dramatic "reskilling" so that
the knowledge worker is "able to exploit the informating capacity of the technology, and to become a new source of critical judgment."[7] Whatever their
purposes, in less than two centuries modern organizations have moved from
oral to print, and finally to electronic authority. In the heavily computer-
mediated environment, however, there are two important changes: a general
requirement of higher intellectual skills, and common access by all members
within an organization to the information produced by the organization, that
is, access to what Zuboff calls the "electronic text."

"The automating capacity of the technology can free the human being for a more comprehensive, explicit, systemic and abstract knowledge of
his or her work made possible by the technology's ability to informate."[8]
"The skills necessary for competent operation in an informated environment
appear to be related to the kind of explicit, inferential, scientific reasoning
traditionally associated with formal education."[9] At the same time, information technology presents several dilemmas in the informated organization. It
can be used to make work more automatic and reduce skill levels, and as a
means for managerial control and observation. At their best, however, information technologies corrode stratified hierarchical organization, make management supervision collaborative, and dramatically increase the responsibility for work of the individual.[10] The result is that the informated organization
needs more smart people operating with initiative and autonomy in an organizational context characterized by teamwork.

Data Gathering—Anthropological Approach

The obstacles to measuring the effects of technological change over time are serious but not insuperable.[11] It is noteworthy that when quantifiable survey techniques are used in similar studies, they are invariably supplemented by some type of structured individual interviews.[12] An attendant problem is the difficulty of establishing large samples across an array of organizations which increases the validity of generalizations. For instance, even in the ten-year time frame of her study, Zuboff assimilated only around 400 individual interviews and about 1,500 pages of notes.[13] Research at UTA resulted in a sample of 35 individuals and 180 pages of typescript responses, which is similar to the results of published research of the type discussed herein.

Studies of organizational behavior in the literature of librarianship predominantly rely on Likert-type surveys. These have the obvious advantages of constraining the respondents to a narrowly defined range of answers which can be conveniently manipulated with statistical packages and subjected to high-level statistical measures. I have, myself, relied on this methodology in my own research. However, when I first began entertaining the notion that Zuboff's findings might be relevant to the library setting, I recognized that her methodology would have to be adapted. Whereas, Zuboff studied several organizations over a ten-year period, the present research focuses on one, The University of Texas at Arlington Libraries, during a four-year period (1987-1991). Zuboff spent a great deal of time as an outsider in these organizations observing the changes which were taking place, discussing those changes with workers, and conducting interviews with those directly affected by automation. Similarly, she explored the perspectives and experiences of mid-level and senior-level managers, as well as technicians in these organizations. Her subjects knew that she was engaged in research which would result in a book, and not a consultant or an employee of the organization. Thus, the research process was "field intensive and longitudinal."[14] So was mine.

In a very real sense I have had the same experience as Zuboff living and working within an organization as its work life was significantly transformed by automation. Obviously, my role was different—not that of an independent researcher objectively interested in organizational change, but as "the boss" subjectively involved in the change. However, my purpose was not unlike Zuboff's—to understand how this automating process affected our organization positively and negatively, and to draw conclusions about how the organization could best adapt to these changes. On the other hand, I could not gather data as she did, since my research was conducted after the automating process was nearly complete. Accordingly, I adopted an approach which would be used by a corporate anthropologist.[15]

Researchers Eveland and Bikson used "highly structured individual interviews . . . [to gather] . . . detailed sociometric data about interactions among group members in addition to information about other aspects of the subjects' work and social lives, attitudes, and evaluation of the task force activity." Like Zuboff, their methodology results in large amounts of narrative data. Data for UTA Libraries was gathered with a survey of twenty-one questions which were designed to elicit narrative responses about the effects of information technology on five general areas: personal work/job assignment, training environment, interpersonal relations, organizational change and decision-making, and service to patrons. The respondents were free to answer as briefly or fully as they wished. Staff were asked to frame their answers to open-ended questions by thinking about "how work was conducted before August 1987, when it was mediated by a paper-file environment" and after that time when changes caused by NOTIS and the LAN were introduced into the UTA Libraries' work environment. Staff respondents were asked to submit their answers anonymously with minimal information about their position and time of original employment.

Data analysis followed the inductive method used by Zuboff. The study of text is a standard activity in the social sciences and humanities. The responses were analyzed to understand the patterns and themes that emerged from the material. Analysis included coding these narrative responses qualitatively, but also the application of quantitative assessment which resulted in nominal data that allows for conclusions about the predominant opinions of the respondents as a group on important matters. The distinctions which are important in how data analysis may be conducted are those between nominal, ordinal, interval, and ratio data. The data used in this study are nominal; that is, there is no measurable difference between the categories; they merely show the presence of a characteristic, such as a favorable opinion towards IT. For such data the only possible statistical applications are simple frequencies and co-occurrence shown in cross-tabulations or contingency tables.[16] The survey was structured to elicit the "range of perspectives on any given issue and to triangulate these perspectives as a way of constructing an image of the organizational system." Quotations included in the text of this research are verbatim and represent the predominant conclusions drawn from the analysis of this data. "They illustrate both the content of thought and the style of expression of the larger group to which the informant belongs."[17]

Only staff members who were employed prior to September 1987 were asked to respond to the survey. This was to ensure that responses came only from those Library employees who experienced the transition to a completely computer-mediated work environment while excluding those who were employed after the automated work environment was already established at UTA Libraries. Of 104 Library staff members, 51, or slightly less than half, were eligible to respond to the survey which was distributed in paper form, but also available for answering on the LAN. LAN stations in the training room or in departments could be used to answer anonymously by e-mail. Handwritten responses were re-keyed before they were analyzed. A return rate of 69 percent (see Table 1) was achieved, and the highest return rate for any group was from people with managerial assignments. However, the response rate among librarians of 69 percent and staff of 59 percent provided a solid basis on which to assess the affects of information technology on staff members working in the

Analysis of Respondents

	JOB ASSIGNMENTS			YEARS OF SERVICE		
Position	Total N Possible*	Respondents N	% Total N	Time of First Employment	N	Percent of Respondents
Assistant/ Associate Directors	5	5	100	1982-87	18	51
Department Heads	6	5	83	1977-81	9	26
Librarians	13	9	69	1972-76	3	9
Staff	27	16	59	Pre-1972	5	14
Total	51	35	69		35	100

*51 of 104 staff were employed by UTA Libraries prior to September 1987 which was the defining criteria for the sample group.

Table 1.

"trenches." Out of 35 respondents, 24 (over 70 percent) were individuals without managerial assignments.

Over half of the respondents (18) were first employed during the five years (1982-87) immediately preceding the beginning of the current automation project. Moreover, 17 of the respondents (49 percent) have worked in UTA Libraries for at least 10 years. Thus, the responding group had the benefit of a long perspective when answering questions concerning change induced by introduction of information technologies. The importance of the insights provided by our experience at the University of Texas at Arlington Libraries is that it is typical, not unique, but therein lies its true value. What is happening at UTA may be helpful to other libraries simply because it establishes a basis for reasonable expectations for this new technology.

Information Technology at UTA

Zuboff's observations for the world of banking, paper manufacture, and the telecommunications industry already could be made about many libraries. The "informating" technologies in libraries include integrated library systems and LANs. After all, the integrated system provides the "electronic text" available to the whole library staff, not to mention patrons, and increases the "intellective" skills and decision-making that library work demands of all staff. Similarly, a LAN with a well-developed management information system, electronic mail, and in-house conferencing capability is a powerful tool for reducing rigidly stratified hierarchy, increasing staff participation and understanding of the organization, making management more approachable, and in general, opening up and flattening the organization. For these things to happen, a conscious decision on the part of managers will still be required. We can choose another path, to use IT for the purpose of increasing authority, hierarchy, and control. To understand the results of the research conducted with our staff requires some description of the IT environment in UTA Libraries, which consist of the Central Library, Architecture and Fine Arts Branch, and the Science and Technology Branch, together serving over 25,000 students and faculty.

The automation experience at UTA Libraries began in 1968 with the introduction of an IBM 357 card-based circulation system. The system was nursed along until 1980, by which time repair visits were being made on almost a daily basis. In 1980, a CLSI LIBS 100 PDP 11 series circulation system was installed, which continued in use until it was replaced in 1988. No significant retrospective conversion of collections to machine-readable form was undertaken during this time. The database used for the CLSI system was comprised largely of records created with initiation of OCLC cataloging of July 1974, and those resulting from "recon" due to use by patrons of books cataloged prior to the introduction of OCLC. Like many libraries, we initiated automation piecemeal in an effort to mechanize specific routine library functions. CLSI served as a stand-alone circulation system. Records were loaded from OCLC cataloging into CLSI with an interface developed by Innovative Interfaces. UTA also utilized the OCLC Acquisition Subsystem. This automation structure required the maintenance of the card catalog. In addition, each of the public services subject divisions then in existence maintained card files for periodicals. In 1984, the subject division units were provided with staff terminals so that they might search the CLSI circulation database. In addition, there were a handful of CLSI terminals available to users. The use of the CLSI Circulation System as a jury-rigged online catalog was very unsatisfactory to patrons and Library staff alike. It was an interim solution.

In 1986, The University of Texas Board of Regents appropriated $1,500,000 for UTA Libraries to initiate a state-of-the-art automation activity. Over the next five years, approximately $2,000,000 total was spent to build the present automation environment. The keystone of this activity was the acquisition and installation of the NOTIS integrated system. Beginning with my first experience in 1981, "NOTIS has always provided an integrated solution by creating a library system that links related records to the MARC bibliographic record resulting in no data redundancy and no need to re-key bibliographic data once it has entered the system. In addition, the most recent status of any item is always reflected in the system allowing staff and patrons to identify an item's current condition at any time. . . . NOTIS also allows you to integrate your online access catalog (OPAC) with other databases not locally at your site."[18] The features of NOTIS are generally known and well documented in the literature.

At the present time, all NOTIS capabilities are operational, including: an online public access catalog which supports a 703,000 record database of all UTA Libraries' LC holdings (OCLC records source), Texas documents, USGPO collection (MARCIVE records source) and a completely barcoded collection with all linked item records established in the system. UTA also maintains the NOTIS Multiple Database Access System (MDAS) and is currently using it for the execution of the U.S. Department of Education Library Technology Grant Study to maintain access to databases extracted from Information Access Corporation files and the ERIC database for the *Current Index to Journals in Education*. As a follow-up to the grant, we are also working with OCLC to develop site-licensed periodical indexing using the OCLC-Faxon Finder databases. This planning focuses on defining and testing a product for which UTA may serve as a development site.

Other NOTIS functions include circulation, fines, fees, and other patron obligations; course reserve, orders of all types, fund accounting, serials check-in, summary holdings for all multi-part items, MARC-based cataloging, and full authority control. The authority control work for the database was processed by Blackwell North America. We have not yet loaded the Library of Congress Subject Heading List which becomes an online interactive file in conjunction with the NOTIS Authority System. UTA also runs the "Generic Transfer and Overlay" which allows records from OCLC to be downloaded for local use. We served as the beta test site for GTO. UTA has systematically acquired new NOTIS subsystems as they have been developed and anticipates participating in the use of the new PACLink product which will allow us to link our NOTIS OPAC with other library sites over the Internet using the Z39.50 and Z39.63 standards. We are maintaining the current version 5.0 of NOTIS and will install enhancements, such as location-based searching and the redesigned serials control subsystem, as soon as they are available. NOTIS at UTA is maintained on a shared IBM 4381 Series 92-E machine running under OS/MVS. The Libraries have acquired 12.5 gigabytes of disk storage for maintaining our databases and other NOTIS activity.

The first fully operational function of NOTIS was cataloging in August 1987. Within twelve months, all other functions were running. Retrospective conversion was completed in late 1988, and the reload of the authority database in early 1989. With the completion of the barcoding and linking of item records in January 1992, all but a few of the tedious database cleanup activities were finished. The NOTIS system is available through the UTA campus network and remotely by dial access locally or over the Internet. We have 43 terminals in our three libraries dedicated to public use and an additional 50 terminals for staff use. In addition, catalogers have hardwired IBM PC-compatible workstations. There are also 61 LAN workstations with Ethernet and/or Procomm mediated access to NOTIS.

In 1988, UTA Libraries began the initiation of our LAN which has matured rapidly. The development of our LAN is best characterized by the adage—"go as far as you can see, and you will be able to see further." The initial intent was to install networked microcomputing for use in the administrative suite by the secretarial pool and senior managers. Once this was done, the purposes of the LAN evolved rapidly because its value was easy to recognize. We presently operate Novell's NetWare 386, Version 3.11. The file server has eight megabytes of RAM and an additional 1.37 gigabytes of disk storage. We employ a four megabyte token ring network in the Central Library which is connected to the two branch libraries with the use of RAD token ring extenders over standard telephone lines. At the present time there are 70 LAN workstations dedicated to staff use. Each of our 40 professional staff has a LAN station in a private office, as do several support staff. All other staff have easy access to at least one LAN station dedicated for their use in the department. An additional six micros are devoted to miscellaneous tasks of system maintenance. We have several generations of PC technology including XT, AT, PS2, and 386 technology. The system supports several networked printers including two Hewlett-Packard laser printers, one an HPIII si. Staff have LAN access to a bank of network modems for dial access to conduct tasks such as online searching and remote access to our "UTA Library Gateway." We are currently experimenting with a software product called SCSI Express to provide LAN access to various CD-ROMs.

It is important to give some consideration to the applications available on the LAN which are used for a variety of management and communication purposes. They are fairly "cutting edge" for libraries. The LAN is mediated primarily by WordPerfect Office 3.0 software. The many applications of the LAN can best be understood by looking at several figures which represent the menus and submenus available over a typical workstation. Figure 1 represents two such screens on the micro at my desk. The user can select any item from the menu and be routed to a submenu or a specific function. For instance, selecting "Management Information System" routes the user to the appropriate submenu. I will return to MIS applications momentarily. The individual user has considerable flexibility in representing what subsystems are available on the main menu, and these are generally tailored to the individual's work style. Depending on RAM capacity, it is possible to bring a number of these applications into operation at one time and to toggle back and forth among them, though we do not use "Windows." Typically, I maintain word processing, calendar, and e-mail simultaneously in RAM.

Turning our attention to a brief review on the first screen, "Agendas" provides access to the public record of past and current agendas for all ad-hoc and working groups. These are viewable, but only the individual "authority" responsible for convening the group may modify agendas. The "Calculator" is self-explanatory. The "Datebook and Appointments" are my individual calendar of daily activities allowing an hour-by-hour scheduling, which is functionally laid out and can provide an audible alert at the station in advance of appointments. "E-mail" has proved to be the single most revolutionary function in WordPerfect Office, allowing for group, as well as individual communications. The "Signout" function was developed from the WordPerfect "Notebook" facility and provides the mechanism for members of a department to indicate their whereabouts. Schedule changes may be entered in advance to maintain a record of anticipated travel or used for daily activities like signout at lunch time. Procomm was the original methodology we used for dial access out of the LAN, but recently we have installed Ethernet connections. "Rolodex" allows me to dial phone numbers automatically through a locally attached modem. The "To-Do Notebook" is a specially designed feature which fits the idiosyncrasies of my work habits and allows me to manage my day-to-day desk work efficiently. Utilities include a variety of functions such as file backup and disk formatting. WordPerfect 5.1 is the current version of our word processing system, and the "Applications" entry takes the user to the submenu screen (Figure 2) which includes a variety of other applications such as DrawPerfect, Ask Sam, LOTUS 1-2-3, Paradox, Procomm, our TCP/IP Ethernet functions, and a Flow Charting system.

I want to turn back briefly to the Management Information System submenu (Figure 1). Our MIS has evolved over the past several years into a mature decision-support system which gives all staff a powerful tool for understanding the work of the Library. "Annual Reports" are provided by the individual departments and summarize the year's work. "Manuals/Help Files" includes system documentation for various applications. "Electronic Publications" represent our first effort at providing access to e-journals obtained through the Internet and stored on the LAN file server. "Goals & Ob-

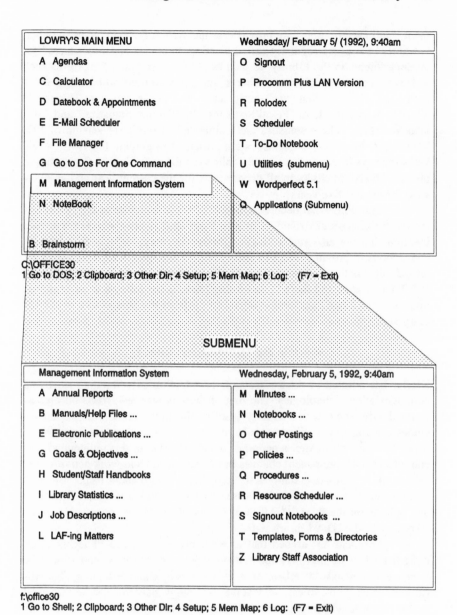

LOWRY'S MAIN MENU	Wednesday/ February 5/ (1992), 9:40am
A Agendas	O Signout
C Calculator	P Procomm Plus LAN Version
D Datebook & Appointments	R Rolodex
E E-Mail Scheduler	S Scheduler
F File Manager	T To-Do Notebook
G Go to Dos For One Command	U Utilities (submenu)
M Management Information System	W Wordperfect 5.1
N NoteBook	Q Applications (Submenu)
B Brainstorm	

C:\OFFICE30
1 Go to DOS; 2 Clipboard; 3 Other Dir; 4 Setup; 5 Mem Map; 6 Log: (F7 = Exit)

SUBMENU

Management Information System	Wednesday, February 5, 1992, 9:40am
A Annual Reports	M Minutes ...
B Manuals/Help Files ...	N Notebooks ...
E Electronic Publications ...	O Other Postings
G Goals & Objectives ...	P Policies ...
H Student/Staff Handbooks	Q Procedures ...
I Library Statistics ...	R Resource Scheduler ...
J Job Descriptions ...	S Signout Notebooks ...
L LAF-ing Matters	T Templates, Forms & Directories
	Z Library Staff Association

f:\office30
1 Go to Shell; 2 Clipboard; 3 Other Dir; 4 Setup; 5 Mem Map; 6 Log: (F7 = Exit)

Figure 1. Management Information System submenu.

jectives" represent the planned year's work for each one of the professional librarians. The "Student/Staff Handbooks" give guidance to the current personnel practices and procedures. Passing over "Library Statistics" for the moment, "Job Descriptions" are provided in the system for every staff member, "Minutes" for every regularly called meeting, "Policies and Procedures" for all departments in the Library, as well as online "Templates" for forms such as leave requests, and fax cover sheets which can be transmitted online by e-mail. The "Library Statistics" entry leads to another submenu (Figure 3) which provides access to "Fiscal Statistics," "Collection Statistics," and "Service Statistics." These statistics are maintained in the LAN version of LO-TUS 1-2-3. However, the statistics are presented in graphic form with a few key strokes as illustrated in Figure 4, allowing the individual staff member to observe levels of activity in all departments for the current year and an overview for the last five years.

This somewhat detailed synopsis conveys a picture of the rich information technology environment in which our staff is now working. I should mention that we also run a "UTA Library Gateway," which uses Internet connections to provide access to other libraries and the CARL UnCover2 database. Information technology has totally changed the working environment at UTA Libraries and there is no turning back. What follows is an examination of how IT has transformed organization from the perspective of the Library staff.

Work in the "Informated" Library

Kiesler has pointed to three effects of the adoption of computers as shared communication technologies. The first of these is planned effects on organizational efficiency, which usually justifies the investment. The second includes organizational adjustments to the new technology, which come to be accepted as the norm after a period of transition. The third is unintended "social effects—the permanent changes in the way social and work activities are organized . . . . Smart executives try to make decisions about technology that win on the first level, minimize losses on the second, and retain flexibility and options on the third."[19] All three orders of effects are observable in the responses of the UTA Library staff.

Ehrmann has argued that assessments of the value of technologies have tended to be narrowly focused on efficiency measures, and should be broadened to include the relationships between people and technology. Specifically, it is reasonable to assume that the technology's success can be measured by the extent to which its users have become positively addicted to its use. "A positive addiction is a practice whose outcomes are beneficial and from which withdrawal would be, at least temporarily, uncomfortable or disabling."[20] We have plenty of evidence to indicate that NOTIS and LAN information technology have created a positive addiction among our staff. Eighty percent describe the change in work environment due to NOTIS as a significant improvement.

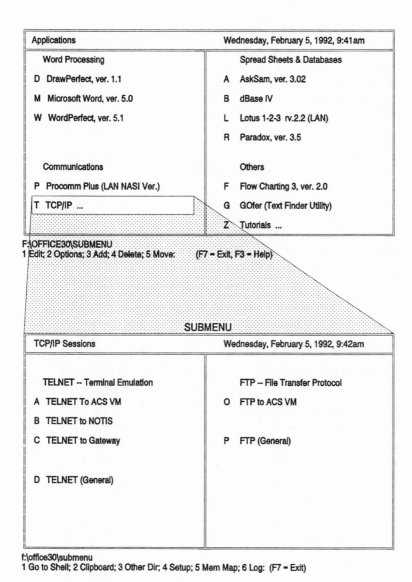

Applications	Wednesday, February 5, 1992, 9:41am
Word Processing	**Spread Sheets & Databases**
D DrawPerfect, ver. 1.1	A AskSam, ver. 3.02
M Microsoft Word, ver. 5.0	B dBase IV
W WordPerfect, ver. 5.1	L Lotus 1-2-3 rv.2.2 (LAN)
	R Paradox, ver. 3.5
Communications	**Others**
P Procomm Plus (LAN NASI Ver.)	F Flow Charting 3, ver. 2.0
T TCP/IP ...	G GOfer (Text Finder Utility)
	Z Tutorials ...

F:\OFFICE30\SUBMENU
1 Edit; 2 Options; 3 Add; 4 Delete; 5 Move: (F7 - Exit, F3 - Help)

SUBMENU

TCP/IP Sessions	Wednesday, February 5, 1992, 9:42am
TELNET -- Terminal Emulation	**FTP -- File Transfer Protocol**
A TELNET To ACS VM	O FTP to ACS VM
B TELNET to NOTIS	
C TELNET to Gateway	P FTP (General)
D TELNET (General)	

f:\office30\submenu
1 Go to Shell; 2 Clipboard; 3 Other Dir; 4 Setup; 5 Mem Map; 6 Log: (F7 - Exit)

Figure 2. "Applications" takes user to the submenu screen.

With a bit of hyperbole, one public services librarian put it this way, "If someone told me that I had my choice between a pay raise with NOTIS keyword searching taken away, or a pay cut with NOTIS keyword searching retained, I would find it very difficult to select the former." A member of our technical

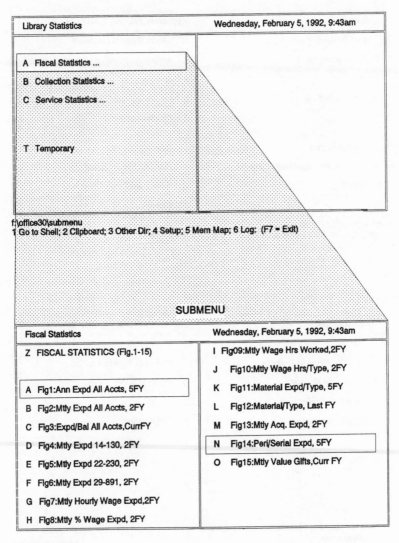

Figure 3. "Library Statistics" leads to another submenu.

services staff says, "My work became more accurate and decisions and actions more easily traced, although more time consuming in early months. NOTIS requires a much more in-depth understanding of the bibliographic records, but it also enables me to make records more accessible."

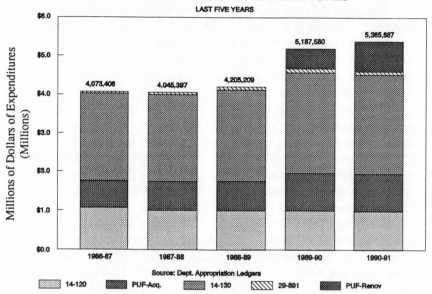

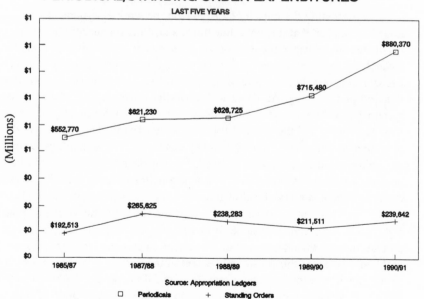

Figure 4. Statistics are presented in graphic form.

One of Zuboff's central conclusions is that IT provides a "transparent" window to the work of the whole organization that increases the level of awareness of the entire work process for all staff who have access to the system. This is certainly borne out by the fact that 63 percent of the sampled staff believe that the presence of IT has increased awareness of work in other departments and of "what is going on" in the Libraries generally. However, I was a bit surprised to find staff responses consistently referring to this quality of transparency and using descriptive phrases in doing so. Repeatedly, terms like "integrated view," "the ability to see," and "our work is no secret anymore," evinced the changed understanding of how we do work in NOTIS. Out of curiosity, I kept a tally and found that fifty percent of the respondents used value-laden phrases to describe the concept of "transparency," and this was more than mere discussion of better access to information. One technical services department head stated, "More people can 'see' what is going on, and more people 'see' what should have been going on. I think this has been positive for the whole Library." A public services librarian observed, "I could always go to their department and learn, but the NOTIS system makes it much easier and more convenient to peek." A classified staff member in technical services put it this way, "Patrons have direct access to files that were formerly invisible to them. This facilitates getting information to them in a timely manner."

Assessing the impact of LAN/IT on the work environment is conditioned by the fact that it is not a functional substitute for specific library tasks conducted in the paper file environment, but rather a new set of information technology tools introduced into a knowledge work environment. As such, LAN/IT supports the work life of the organization, but requires new ways of thinking and working. As Kraut and others have shown ". . . the computer system had different effects depending on worker's job category, the tasks they performed, and the types of offices they worked in. They also caused us to challenge our assumption of one-way causation. The technology evolved as workers used it in innovative ways."[21] Together with NOTIS, the LAN presents a shared environment in which data is immediately available to everyone and there is a high level of interpersonal communication which allows for the evaluation of information and keeps the entire Library staff up to date and focused on organizational performance. In some ways the data is less important, though, than the impact of the system on communications and shared problem solving. In this regard, 67 percent of the staff took time to make very strong positive responses about specific capabilities of the LAN discussed earlier. A typical response comes from one member of our classified staff in technical services:

LAN/IT makes it faster and easier to compose minutes of meetings. Right procedures for jobs, compose letters to gift patrons, and send messages to all the various members of the different councils when I need to. The spreadsheet capabilities on the LAN/IT make it easy and quick to do my monthly reports. The mailing label capabilities make it easy to get the reports ready to be mailed out. Instead of typing a hundred different addresses, all it takes is a couple of simple commands to print all the address labels needed from my WordPerfect file.

A public services librarian of over fifteen years experience pulled no punches. "To be very honest, I started out with a pretty hefty negative attitude regarding the LAN. I knew it was costing us big bucks, and it seemed like a luxury we couldn't afford. After a brief period of time, however, the benefits became obvious. I believe the communication improvement alone is probably worth the cost." Those respondents discussing the LAN communications all were positive about the capability, and the majority made strong statements concerning the way in which the LAN has fundamentally changed communications in libraries. It is, however, curious that a substantial number (31 percent) expressed a lament that the use of LAN for communications might be reducing interpersonal contact. At the same time, a similar number stated with almost the exact same phraseology "I don't have to play telephone tag anymore." This concern about possible decline in personal contact may prove to be unfounded, since a controlled study of e-mail groups "confirm[s] that those in the electronic task force think they have formed significantly more lasting social ties than those in the standard condition."[22]

When asked how information technology is affecting their individual job assignments, most respondents focused on the improved efficiency with which they worked. A substantial majority (63 percent) expressed the view that their work-related decision-making was easier or reflected increased consultation. Over 74 percent of the responding staff strongly emphasized the constant and higher level of "awareness" of information technology which was needed to do the job in the new environment. A public services librarian of fifteen years experience stated it this way, "I have been forced to upgrade my abilities with computers because of the NOTIS LAN/IT . . . . I have come to regard increasing my efficiency with computers as an ever-present desirable aspect of what I will need to know to do my job well." A clerical staff member in technical services described it similarly, "Greater knowledge of computer technology is required because of the need to move around in all the different subsystems and applications. You have to be very flexible and ready to learn . . . . Also, if you are very knowledgeable, you have a tendency to be asked for help a lot." Statements like these underscore that one of Zuboff's most important insights is true in UTA Libraries. Smart machines require more smart people, and a learning environment is emerging which involves a great majority of staff.

There are benefits to the library which arise from such an environment, particularly if full utilization of IT by all staff levels can be ensured. Lawrence Young has pointed out that "While we have seen a dramatic increase in the use of interactive computer support systems by managers and staff professionals in coping with semi-structured decision situations, these systems have not generally been made accessible to workers for identifying work method improvements, except in a few leading-edge companies."[23] In this sense, libraries may be more "leading edge" than other components of higher education. Oberg's recent study of the requirements for para-professional staff indicated that "a number of higher-level skills and competencies are required of para-professionals in a high percentage of libraries surveyed. For example, computer skills are required of all or some para-professionals by 96 percent of the responding ARL and by 93 percent of responding Carnegie sample libraries." Similarly, he concluded that the "collective portrait of para-professionals that emerges from this survey is that of a vital growing force within academic libraries. Few traditional or newly created tasks are off limits, and they are routinely assigned complex duties that a generation ago characterized the work of librarians." One would infer that the professional content of the work that librarians do is also increased by this trend as more routine tasks are moved downward in the organization largely because of the impact of information technology.[24]

Comments from two of the staff give a qualitative "feel" for the general transformation that IT has caused for everyone working in our Libraries. One public services para-professional views changes in personal work assignments in this way:

> The work itself seems to be simpler, but the process of work, i.e., the means by which the actual work is done, has become far more complex. The proliferation of steps, procedures, and policies, has increased working time. The number of tasks has also increased. The presence of automation itself creates work. In fact, there would be no need, reason, or way to do some of the work which is done if NOTIS did not exist. For example, the MARCIVE tapeloads have created an electronic raison d'etre for much of what I do. NOTIS is better, but a paper shelflist is much simpler. Additionally, NOTIS has essentially reshaped my entire job description. The landscape of the department and its workflow were drastically altered by it. NOTIS pulled us from the Stone Age to the Space Age, in effect.

A department head took the following broad view of change in our Libraries' work life:

Certainly one positive aspect would be a much greater "inclusion aspect" of my job, in that so much previously contained, super difficult to locate information is now public knowledge and it is easier for me to gauge whether I am "in step" with the cadence of the various levels of the organization. That is to say, a closer identification with the personality of the library and a greater feeling of confidence with the role I perform within it. So very much of the organization's work has been demystified and certainly better understood based upon this current awareness and closer cooperation required of all.

Organization, Decision-Making, and the Collaborative Imperative

Historical parallels for the social change caused by technological innovation are many—the medieval castle, the printed book, and the automobile. These inventions stimulated change similar to the dramatic social transformation caused by the informating power of information technologies. But the most important change caused by the latter "is the increased intellectual content of work tasks across organizational levels that attenuate the conventional designations of manager and managed. This does not mean that there are no longer useful distinctions to be made among organizational members, but whatever these distinctions may be, they will no longer convey fundamentally different modes of involvement with the life of the organization . . . . Instead, the total organizational skill base becomes more homogenous."[25]

Traditional hierarchical organizations have narrow spans of control and many reporting levels. Moreover, the quality of expertise increases as one moves up the hierarchy and is held closely by specialists and managers. In the informated organization, on the other hand, expertise and information often reside in software and anyone who has access to the system may become an expert. In addition, as systems are networked expertise and information is distributed more evenly throughout the organization. By definition, networking overcomes the limitations of geography and hierarchy, allowing communications across both. "Networks will not replace or supplement hierarchies; rather, the two will be encompassed within a broader conception that embraces both."[26]

Today there are five billion telephones in the United States, serving a population of 260,000,000, about nineteen each for every man, woman and child in the country. "When the telephone was invented, everyone thought that it would serve businesspeople primarily . . . . Technical innovations have more effects than most people realize, and the same is true of the computer. What many managers regarded as merely a tool for storing and transmitting information has social effects that can be more important in the long run. Because computers break down hierarchies and cut across norms and organization boundaries, people behave differently when using them. And once the social context is altered, the organization changes."[27] Tom Peters has observed that "hierarchy is, it turns out, all about information and the power that comes from controlling it—nothing more."[28] The conclusion one draws from this notion is that the information technology revolution is transforming the very basis for power within organizations. Perin expresses concern that the change implied in "groupware such as electronic mail, conferencing, and online editing . . . . [which] . . . . has an apparently natural affinity to the team and project work of salaried professional employees" may be resisted because "managers find it difficult to acknowledge the value of autonomy and self-management."[29] The responses of the UTA staff underscore both the dilemmas and opportunities that are presented by these organizational changes.

Our staff clearly believe that the personal work relationships within their departments have been affected by information technology. Fifty-seven percent would characterize that change as making the relationship more interdependent, cohesive, and communicative. Over 46 percent felt that the changed work environment also required closer working relationships between themselves as individuals and other departments. A public services librarian employed for over fifteen years at UTA gave this assessment, "Without the LAN, I think we would feel more distant and less united since our offices are spread out and our desk schedules often keep us from seeing each other for extended periods. Sometimes we banter as if we were in the same room sharing funny stuff over the LAN. We will allow ourselves to be more spontaneous through the LAN than over a telephone or in written communication. Almost as good as being in person." Similarly, a technical services librarian wrote "I [previously] had a close working relationship with the corresponding bibliographers in my subject areas. These relationships have been intensified as I can more immediately explain and solve problems for them while we are speaking on the telephone and both of us are looking at the same information on our terminals."

Research has indicated that the nature of supervision also frequently undergoes a shift in the informating process. Of the respondents, 29 percent indicated that there was no perceived change in the way a department was supervised. But over half described supervision as more consultative, requiring an environment characterized by communication, learning, and teaching—a "together environment." Fifty-one percent also stated that their personal relationships with the supervisor had become either more positive or characterized by improved communication. Two public services librarians viewed it this way—"It is a constant learning environment, and I am most grateful for that," and "a more open style of communication . . . seems to fit in with the NOTIS LAN/IT."

In the midst of this organizational transformation of work relationships, there is one very curious set of results from the staff survey, which relates to the departmental organization of UTA Libraries. Concurrent with the introduction of NOTIS and LAN/IT, we also undertook significant reorganization of the two largest units—Public Services and Technical Services which was ultimately renamed Collections and Bibliographic Services. The reorganization of Technical Services explicitly took into account issues of workflow in the integrated environment of NOTIS. However, only slightly over 28 percent of the responding staff felt that the reorganization of Technical Services was caused by automation. Where Public Services was concerned, no respondents felt that reorganization was driven by the automating process. In fact, 37 percent explicitly said that it was not. In general, 60 percent of the responding staff who bothered to answer felt that the presence of these two information technologies supported but did not cause the departmental reorganizations. One would conclude that staff believe other departmentalization would be possible, and that on the whole, another organization might do as well.

Michael Schrage has hit upon the key difference that will characterize these new types of informated organizations—a high level of collaboration within the organization. He believes that one of the primary characteristics of information technology and the electronic text is as a tool for collaboration, both in meetings and across the organization on a continuous basis.[30] When we invest in information technology as a solution, "we need to shift away from the notion of technology managing information and toward the idea of technology as a medium of relationships. Organizations need to get a better understanding of the complex ecologies of media that shape, deflect, and define one another."[31] However, collaboration is not a cure-all but has specific ingredients that define the organizational ways in which it may be useful:

- *Competence*—Individual collaborators must at least be competent to deal with the problem they face.

- *A shared, understood goal*—Collaboration is treated as a means to an end, not an end in itself.

- *Mutual respect, tolerance, and trust*—The collaboration exists precisely because the collaborators believe they need one another to get the job done.

- *Creation and manipulation of "shared spaces"* —Shared space is essential as a technique to achieve conversational clarity and includes old-fashioned blackboards, flip charts, and new collaborative technologies, such as e-mail, bulletin boards, conferencing systems, and electronic blackboards.

- *Multiple forms of representation* —Collaborations generally use a variety of forms of expression which may include mathematics, linguistics, structural representations, conversational, and visual representation which allow the collaborators to grasp the key features of the task.

- *Playing with the representations* —Play here connotes playful and implies that participants do not have to commit to anything until they feel ready to do so.

- *Continuous but not continual communication* —Collaborators contact one another based on the need to resolve problems, not meet organizational requirements.

- *Formal and informal environments* — Classic collaboration occurs in numerous formal and informal settings and is capable of surviving the change of scenery.

- *Clear lines of responsibility but no restricted boundaries* —Everyone remains responsible for their own duties, but each is encouraged to create a common understanding of the entire task.

- *Decisions do not have to be made by a consensus* —Collaboration is used as a tool to collectively generate the ideas which resolve the problem, but it does not imply consensus.

- *Physical presence is not necessary* —This has always been true to some extent but is increasingly so in the electronic environment.

- *Selected use of outsiders for complementary insights and information* —The collaborative group chooses when to go outside of itself to obtain vital information to stimulate the creative process.

- *Collaborations end* —Long-term successful collaborations are rare. Because they are purposeful collaborations of necessity, they eventually come to an end.[32]

The obvious application of this notion of collaboration in the informated library is to resolve internal organizational problems and meet organizational goals, and this will happen frequently. Indeed, Eveland and Bikson in some measure both believe that collaboration is imperative, perhaps inevitable.

> When a web of interactive technology is introduced into a work
> group, the sociotechnical system is altered; work groups increasingly become directly dependent on their material means and resources for their output. That is to say, individuals become interdependent not only on one another but also on the technology for
> accomplishing their tasks; access to and control over the means
> of production assume greater importance. New communication
> channels can introduce new ways of productive interaction; they
> can also exacerbate existing differences and force confronta-
> tions.[33]

Their research indicates that "the electronic task force" interacts more effectively, is easier to coordinate, and can undertake fairly ambitious and substantial efforts involving a larger number of people and complete the tasks with greater speed than groups working in more traditionally organized environments. E-groups also demonstrate more leadership flexibility with different individuals emerging depending on the nature of the task, as well as substantially more satisfaction with the results of the group's work. Finally, it seems that such groups are more socially integrated at the end of the task than are standard groups.[34]

What does the survey of UTA Library staff tell us about this matter of group work and decision-making? We have already observed that staff understand that the greater sharing of information through this system provides them with knowledge that they did not have previously, and this knowledge has a direct effect on the decision-making process. Sixty-three percent of responding staff indicated that the decision-making dimension of their job had changed, becoming easier but requiring more consultation. A support staff member in Public Services has this view: "Whereas I used to make my own little decisions about how to do certain things, I find that procedural decisions must be standardized because of NOTIS . . . and the needs of other system users." A member of the Technical Services support staff believes that "IT has made me more accountable for decisions as I have access to more information. It is also easier to get input from other departments in making decisions." Even senior-level administrators feel there has been a change. An assistant director stated that, "I find I am often brought into discussions and consulted on issues that in the past might have excluded me because of the ease of direct and multiple communication."

The conclusions of staff concerning departmental decision-making are not so clear cut, perhaps because the question asked for an opinion on how IT had affected participation in routine decision-making. Many felt that no change in *who* made routine decisions had occurred, but 43 percent indicated paradoxically that NOTIS required greater participation in the decisions of their departments. Forty percent also felt that the LAN abetted participation and dissemination of decisions. By contrast, 60 percent of the respondents indicated that NOTIS required much more consultation between departments. A member of the Public Services staff contends that "Such freedom is probably extinct by now. The NOTIS environment will not allow that kind of independence. By its very nature, NOTIS compels us to coordinate our activities between departments." A member of the Technical Services clerical staff saw it this way, "There seems to be now a general awareness that if one individual department changes procedures without informing others, there is the possibility for chaos to occur. The willingness of one department to inform others of their change in practices is quite evident. Now when a department changes a procedure they usually [send a] LAN [message to] all interested departments. The new procedures are always made available on the LAN."

Senior administrators would seem to be the one group whose power to make decisions independently would be the least circumscribed by the new work environment. Yet, when asked about this, few staff (11 percent) indicated that their freedom had not been restricted, and 69 percent felt that the greater information required to make decisions had increased the level of participation required before senior administrators could make decisions. Even if we remove senior managers from the tally, 54 percent of the respondents stated that their freedom to make decisions was restricted. A clerical staff member in Technical Services observed, "IT has now made them more aware of how their decisions affect workers. It is now quite easy for them to ask for input on various changes that are proposed (and they usually do). When they do ask for staff's input on these changes, it does create a more positive work environment." One Public Services librarian made the remark," I would say that it has unequivocally had the opposite effect, that of making it virtually unheard of for there to be no prior consultation in major decisions." Senior administrators feel much the same themselves. One indicated that "information technology has democratized decisions. More input is sought from people both vertically and horizontally throughout the organizational structure of the Library."

Frequently terms like collegial, collaboration, teamwork, and interdependence drift into the language used to respond to the questions about decision-making in the libraries. A Public Services librarian probably characterized it best, "I feel that we work together in a team-like environment, but I don't know to what extent the NOTIS/IT is responsible." In fact, around 17 percent of the responding staff indicated that the climate of consultation was more a matter of intentional management practice than a function of the growth of information technology. One observed that, "In the early years of IT in this Library, it was made clear that participation, while welcome and needed, was very much a real part or requirement of a professional's job. All the . . . IT in the world is not a substitute for a managerial climate which fosters and encourages this participation." What these differences of perception point to is a conclusion drawn by Zuboff, that management practice of consultation, group work and decision-making is reciprocal with information technology. They may interact and reinforce one another. To put it in the simplest of terms, one may hope that the massive introduction of information technology at UTA Libraries has presented us with an opportunity to fulfill a goal of greater participation by all staff in decision-making. It is that kind of work environment which recognizes that every member of the staff has a brain.

There is another not so obvious, but equally important dimension of collaboration in the new library paradigm which Peter Drucker has referred to obliquely. "The greatest need is to look at a different role for the information provider, the librarian. Information resources are changing so fast that the librarian in the academic and research laboratory is at the beginning of a partnership with the faculty and researcher. Neither side has taken full responsibility for this partnership. . . . It is the librarian who knows the information resources and needs to be in on the planning of every research program."[35] Amitai Etzioni has made a similar point. "For information to be turned into knowledge requires collaboration with other disciplines. . . . But if librarians would see themselves as knowledge managers and work together with other disciplines such as medicine, economics, sociology, physics—they would go a long way toward ensuring that the knowledge systems would be set up in such a way that they would make it easier to move from masses of unprocessed information to a specific number of conclusions."[36]

What did we learn in the UTA survey concerning staff perceptions about the ways in which information technology is affecting the information exchange between us and the Libraries' patrons? Of the responding group, 57 percent indicated that the most significant change was that the integrated system opened up the entire library and its technical processes to the patron. This high level of response should be underscored because many of the respondents do not have any regular contact with patrons. One reference librarian stated that, "The keyword searching capability of NOTIS has opened up a whole new way of helping patrons seek what they need. This is a concrete way that NOTIS has affected my interaction with patrons. They are grateful for the system, especially those faculty members and graduate students who were here before NOTIS. I think that Library users' attitudes toward the whole Library have become more favorable because we now have a fairly user-friendly system and all materials are represented in it." Forty-six percent of the staff stated the same positive response from patrons in various ways.

Among the staff responding to the survey, there was one cohort (nine or 26 percent of the sample) composed of Public Services librarians and support staff working with patrons as a significant and continuous part of their assignment. All but one of this group commented pointedly on the fact that the new environment requires much more time in user education. One Reference librarian commented, "More and more I find myself teaching Library patrons about the variety of computer systems available to them at the UTA Library and how to use those systems. Very often I am either doing it for the patron, or walking them through the procedure." Some of the comments were expressions of concern at the impact of this new responsibility on reference desk work, while others were frankly excited about this new interaction with patrons. This change is so clearly perceived that it bears careful consideration. Certainly, before the introduction of information technology we spent a great deal of time helping patrons navigate the old subject divisional arrangement, similarly teaching them about print indexes and the various card catalogs. It is paradoxical, then, that there is such a clear expression that the new environment requires more user education. There must be a qualitative change related to the introduction of information technology as part of a new expectation about the interaction between Public Services staff and patrons. Moreover, this expanded educational role that librarians will play in the mediation of complex new information technologies may only be expected to increase in importance. I think it will also lead to the further development of the collaborative relationship between librarians as the mediators of information resources, and patrons as the consumers.

If librarians are to truly enter into the necessary collaborations, then it is time to abandon the notion that the role of librarians and libraries is to passively provide the basic information to patrons without a serious concern for judging the quality of what is provided. This is a tricky matter since it involves a core principle of the profession embodied in the American Library Association and Association of American Publishers joint statement, "The Freedom To Read." We must continue to build broad-based collections that provide the full diversity of ideas and expressions of opinion, not some orthodoxy. However, along with the responsibility of the profession to provide access to the whole of the record of knowledge is a new responsibility, one that Wilson calls "a true information service . . . . Such a service would accept inquiries in the form of statements of a problem and respond with a description of what is presently known that bears on the solution of the problem. It would explicitly undertake to vouch for the accuracy of the information given as being part of the public knowledge, and would deliberately attempt to provide only such information as was of probable utility in the solution of the problem or the improvement of a decision situation."[37] It could be stated in this way—that librarians must abandon a studied neutrality concerning the access to knowledge we provide since in many cases it is already an insupportable fiction. This means that we must explicitly begin to make judgements about the message *in the* medium, whenever we are asked to do so.

If information technology has the organizational effect of breaking down hierarchy, then it must also contribute to building a collaborative process. Collaboration will become an organizational imperative both within and without the library. Within the library it will be focused on infrastructure work by staff. Without, it will involve assisting the information seeker. Collaborative work will also involve the mediation of information technologies, and it will be different from what has traditionally been viewed as teamwork.

Training—Transforming the Hierarchy

We come now to the issue of training, which Zuboff ties directly to the "post-hierarchical period of industrial organization," which will be characterized by, "empowering the front lines with information, intellective skills, and the opportunity to act on what they can learn [that] requires, in turn, new forms of roles and relationships, particularly where the role of middle management is concerned." "But how do we create such organizations where the principal axis of human behavior shifts from control and obedience to teaching and learning?"[38] One of the organizational assumptions that has stood as an obstacle to this shift in the role of managers is that they are somehow different from the people they manage. In the past this was in some measure true, since managers possessed information that others usually did not and were, therefore, "uniquely equipped to deal with information and for that reason we granted them authority."[39] "People are going to be working together more and more to make sense out of abstraction which puts a premium on group interaction and problem solving. We need managers who are skilled in creating a social environment where this can flourish."[40]

> For managers who participate in this psychological context, it is difficult to share knowledge or to be concerned with helping their subordinates to learn. First, this implies that workers can learn what the managers know, thus calling into question of the necessity of managerial authority. Second, it implies that workers need to understand in order to execute, which is affront to the collective faith that keeps a hierarchy afloat. Persuasion, influence, education—these are not easily compatible with the beliefs necessary to maintain imperative control.[41]

We've already seen the strong sense in our responding group that decision-making has become more participative. This implies directly a changing role for managers. But the picture that emerges from the comments of our respondents indicates we have a way to go at UTA Libraries before we develop the collaborative training environment Zuboff envisions. One assistant director described learning the LAN in this way, "I'm largely self-taught, though I've learned in bits and pieces by consulting with a variety of other people as the need arose. I did attend the introduction to the LAN offered by Jian and learned a few new things. As people have put out information through the LAN itself about how to perform certain skills, I have copied their instructions, then practiced until I had mastered the skill. I've also offered basic instruction to my own department heads in carrying out certain operations that I have asked them to perform in the course of communicating through the LAN." A department head described our training this way, "Formal training for NOTIS implementation was required, and to my way of thinking, well delivered. Formal training for subsequent upgrades and releases is required and has been practically non-existent. Judging from the questions that I receive from new Public Services librarians, they need formal NOTIS training to get them to a point of being able to interpret the data being presented." On the other hand, a member of the classified staff states that "NOTIS/IT was easy to learn and use. There was sufficient documentation and training to get us ready to use NOTIS/IT." But perhaps the most characteristic statement comes from another Technical Services staff member who states, "More technical knowledge is required. I need to know IT well to train others, and although I know much more than I ever did, I still feel inadequate when reading some of the memos, minutes, and LAN messages. [This is true of] NOTIS and upgrades in OCLC. I'm in a position to train others in these functions, but still need more myself."

If this series of quotes seems confusing, so were the array of responses to the questions concerning both formal and informal training. No staff consensus emerged on whether formal training or the way it was sought had changed, improved, or gotten worse. There is a clear recognition that we made a significant effort at formal training with the implementation of NOTIS and that we have hired a trainer for our microcomputing environment. There was considerable comment concerning the shared informal training that has emerged in the LAN environment, but that does not seem to be recognized as an integral part of our concept of training. There is, however, a preponderant body of opinion on one fact. Over 62 percent of the respondents took the time to state in one fashion or another that we need more and continuous training, in short, a thoroughgoing set of practices that relate to improving their understanding of how our information technology works.

Clearly, we have much to do with respect to developing a training culture, but much is to be gained by improving staff effectiveness and thus gaining the greatest benefit from our investment in information technology. "Those not engaged in front-line activity must be active as educators and integrators. They help develop intellective skills at the front line. They manage the social system in order to create the conditions of collegiality in which the joint problem solving and discursiveness, so vital in the informated organization, can flourish."[42]

Conclusions

A friend and colleague is fond of saying that "The great libraries of the future will not be those with great collections, but those with great staffs." Why is this so? Simply because knowledge must be rediscovered in the library in order to be used and that process of rediscovery may be as important as the creation of knowledge itself. Patrons have always sought the assistance of librarians in this search to rediscover. In the "virtual" library of the future, a new more vital, and certainly a more challenging role, awaits the profession that emerges within the new paradigm as the mediator of knowledge. What profession should that be if not librarianship?

Managing an informated library suggests different approaches, but the outlines of what this organization will require may only be inferred since it is just now taking shape. Above all, staff will be working in the same "electronic text" and this will mean that knowledge about the organization will be more fully shared. Who is the expert in such settings when shared knowledge means that hierarchy no longer defines expertise? How will such an organization make its decisions, when managers no longer monopolize key information? Moreover, the informated library will demand a dramatic "reskilling" of the knowledge workers it employs. What will they demand of the organization—a role in decision-making, higher wages, flatter hierarchies, autonomy and control over their work environment? The challenges of managing an informated library will be numerous. The imperative of training will take on added dimensions and will transcend "traditional" supervision. Lines of authority and spans of control will become amorphous, and the matrix organization will take on new meaning. External relationships with patron groups will shift and the notion of service will be attenuated by the concept of collaboration. The sense of library as "place" will be diluted, though it will not disappear. Library will also become process.

Notes

1. See for instance, Duane Webster, "Organizational Futures: Staffing Research Libraries in the 1990's," in Minutes of the Association of Research Libraries, Oc-

tober 24-25, 1984 (Washington, D.C., Association of Research Libraries); Robert C. Heterick, Jr., "Networked Information: What Can We Expect and When?," *CAUSE/EFFECT* 13, no. 2 (Summer 1990): 9-14; and Robert C. Heterick, Jr., "Academic Sacred Cows and Exponential Growth," *CAUSE/ EFFECT* 14, no. 1 (Spring 1991): 9-13. The author has developed this theme in two articles, see, Charles B. Lowry, "Converging Information Technologies: How Will Libraries Adapt?," *CAUSE/EFFECT* 13, no. 3 (Fall 1990): 35; and Charles B. Lowry, "Information Technologies and the Transformation of Libraries and Librarianship," *The Serials Librarian* 21, no. 2/3 (1991), 109-32. The first of these two articles discuss the author's views on how information technologies will be used by libraries and library patrons. The second is a preliminary investigation of the "informating" effects of IT, which discusses ways in which information technologies will affect library work, organization, and education, and librarianship as a profession. The present article is, in effect, an extension of this earlier work, which uses anthropological methodology to investigate the "informating" processes in The University of Texas at Arlington Libraries.

2. Margaret Masterman, "The Nature of a Paradigm," in *Criticism and the Growth of Knowledge: Proceedings of the International Colloquium in the Philosophy of Science, London, 1965, volume 4*, ed. by Imre Lakatos and Alan Musgrave, (Cambridge: University Press, 1970), 59-89.

3. Charles Martell, "Mysteries, Wonders, and Beauties," editorial in *College and Research Libraries* 51, no. 3 (May 1990): 179.

4. Ray Kurzweil, *The Age of Intelligent Machines* (Boston: Massachusetts Institute of Technology, 1990), 328.

5. Charles B. Lowry, "An Interview With Peter Drucker," *Library Administration and Management* 4, no. 1 (Winter 1989): 3-5.

6. Shoshana Zuboff, *In the Age of the Smart Machine: The Future of Work and Power* (New York: Basic Books, Inc., Publishers, 1988), xiii, 9-10.

7. Ibid., 23, 57, 62-63, 69-70.

8. Ibid., 77-79, 114, 126, 179-81.

9. Ibid., 195.

10. Ibid., 243, 285, 287, 290-91, 296-97, 303, 308-10.

11. Robert Kraut, Susan Dumais, and Susan Koch, "Computerization, Productivity, and Quality of Work-Life," *Communications of the ACM*, 32, no. 2 (February 1989): 223-27.

12. Ibid., 228; J. D. Eveland and T. K. Bikson, "Work Group Structures and Computer Support: A Field Experiment," *ACM Transactions on Office Information Systems*, 6, no. 4 (October 1988): 357.

13. Ellen Benoit, "Programming a Personal Future," *Forbes* (May 23, 1983): 77-78; see also Eveland, 358.

14. Zuboff, *In the Age of the Smart Machine*, 225-26, 422-28.

15. See for instance, Jennifer J. Laabs, "Corporate Anthropologists," *Personnel Journal*, 71, no. 1 (January 1992): 81-91.

16. For a succinct discussion of the significance of levels of data, see Norman H. Nie, et al., *SPSS: Statistical Package for the Social Sciences* (2nd ed., New York: McGraw-Hill, 1975), 4-6.

17. Zuboff, *In the Age of the Smart Machine*, 428-29.

18. NOTIS Systems, Incorporated, Marketing and Sales Group, *NOTIS Solutions: Expanding Your Library's Resources* (Evanston, Illinois: NOTIS Systems, Incorporated, 1991): 2.

19. Sara Kiesler, "The Hidden Messages in Computer Networks," *Harvard Business Review*, 64, no. 1 (January-February, 1986): 46.
20. Stephen C. Ehrmann, "Gauging the Educational Value of A College's Investments in Technology," *Educom Review* (Fall/Winter 1991): 26.
21. Kraut, 221.
22. Eveland, 375.
23. Lawrence Young, "Decision Support Systems for Workers: A Bridge to Advancing Productivity," *Information & Management*, 16, no. 3 (1989): 132.
24. Larry R. Oberg, "The Role, Status, and Working Conditions of Paraprofessionals: A National Survey of Academic Libraries," *College and Research Libraries*, (forthcoming 1992). The author wishes to thank Mr. Oberg, who provided a copy of the prepublication manuscript for purposes of this chapter.
25. Zuboff, *In the Age of the Smart Machine*, 388-93.
26. Stanley M. Davis, *Future Perfect* (Reading, Massachusetts: Addison-Wesley Publishing Company, Inc., 1987), 24, 80-81, 86-90.
27. Kiesler, 46.
28. Tom Peters, "The Destruction of Hierarchy," *Industry Week*, 230 (August 15, 1988): 33.
29. Constance Perin, "Electronic Social Fields in Bureaucracies," *Communications of the ACM*, 34, no. 12 (December 1991): 75, 78.
30. Michael Schrage, *Shared Minds: The New Technologies of Collaboration* (New York: Random House, 1990), 6, 7, 96-134.
31. Ibid., 142.
32. Ibid., 135-63.
33. Eveland, 355.
34. Ibid., 355, 358, 365-68, 372, 375.
35. Charles B. Lowry, "An Interview With Peter Drucker," *Library Administration and Management* 4, no. 1 (Winter 1989): 4.
36. Charles B. Lowry, "An Interview With Amitai Etzioni," *Library Administration and Management* 4, no. 1 (Winter 1989): 7; this theme of collaboration between librarians and researchers also appears in William D. Earvey, *Communications: The Essence of Science* (Oxford: Pergamon Press Ltd., 1979), 10-12, 126.
37. Wilson, *Public Knowledge*, 109-10, 121-23; Wilson makes a similar case in *Shared Knowledge*, 165-96.
38. Shoshana Zuboff, "Informate the Enterprise, An Agenda for the Twenty-First Century," *Phi Kappa Phi Journal*, 71, no. 3 (Summer 1991): 6.
39. Shoshana Zuboff, "Smart Machines, Smart People," *Inc*, 11, no. 1 (January 1989): 32.
40. Roxane Farmanfarmaian, "Four Women Who've Seen the Future," *Working Woman*, 13 (November 1988): 84.
41. Zuboff, *In the Age of the Smart Machine*, 250.
42. Zuboff, "Informate the Enterprise," 7.

The New Service Frontier: Electronic Full-Text and the Macrostructure of Information

Paul M. Gherman

The possibility of offering full-text electronic information draws closer and closer. New electronic journals are appearing almost monthly, and OCLC and AAAS have announced an electronic journal with graphics and hypertext which they hope will be a "cookie cutter" model for many more electronic journals. Technical difficulties remain. Most electronic journals are ASCII text only, without graphics or the sophistication of page layout equal to print. Other journals use scanned images which combine text and image; however, they are difficult to display in standard terminals, cannot be easily indexed to the word level, and take massive amounts of storage. These technical difficulties will be overcome in the near future, and when they are, we can expect to see a rapid explosion of electronic publication.

Electronic full-text publication, when combined with powerful new nation-wide or even world-wide telecommunication networks, differs so markedly from print media that it will bring a total restructuring of what is known as the scholarly communication process. The relationship between author, publisher, library, and reader will be forever changed, and the institutions and methods created over the last several hundred years will be fundamentally changed. This chapter explores the various models which could be established as the current players develop the virtual library of tomorrow and consider their impact on the role and services to be offered by libraries.

Although we have been using networks such as OCLC for twenty years, many of us have only recently seen the implementation of campus networks which extend libraries beyond their walls. Many university library OPACs are available across campus and beyond. Other services such as remote ILL requests, book ordering, and reference services are now offered that allow students and faculty to access the library from offices, dorm rooms, and homes. Still, these services have had little impact on the mission or role of libraries which have continued to concentrate on bibliography. Tomorrow's virtual library of full-text information will shake the very foundations of the profession of librarianship as well as the lives of all users and purveyors of information.

The Virtual Library

Over the last two to three years, new developments have occurred with increasing frequency and intensity; namely, the Internet or NREN has become rich with a wide variety of information resources. Libraries are very active participants in this activity; however, much is happening without library involvement. E-mail, bulletin boards, government databases, listservs on almost any imaginable topic, newsletters, and electronic journals are but a few of the new kinds of information resources appearing daily on the "net." Over 150 OPACs are accessible via the Internet, many from libraries in other countries. It is this change—especially the development of full-text information—that has the potential to change the very nature of our libraries, if not to spell the end of libraries as we have known them. The creation of the virtual library is at hand.

Presently there is a confused concept or definition of a virtual library, and until it becomes a reality no specific description can be made. At best it might be described as: *information existing at a limited number of locations on the Internet, but almost universally accessible, and with the presentation of that information to the user as though it were local and unified via directory services.* Therefore, in the future, most libraries will present a wide universe of information to their users as though that information were local, instead of the current practice of presenting a subset of locally held, available information to the patron. The virtual library will represent the end shift of the paradigm where access will be universal and ownership very limited. As we move toward the virtual library, major shifts in the traditional roles of authors, publishers, indexers, libraries, and even readers will occur.

Authors

The creation of information begins with authors who synthesize the work of others, add new interpretations to existing information, and create new knowledge. Authors own their work to begin with; however, to assure its distribution, archiving and preservation, they generally relinquish rights to their work. In the virtual library, it is conceivable that authors could retain control of their work and also assume the distribution, archiving, and preservation of that work. The work could exist at the personal network address of each author, available to readers everywhere. Stephen King could maintain his works on his personal computer on the net, available by FTP to each reader for a price. He could pay a fee to the directory provider to list his address or works on the net, or he might not pay at all. "White Pages" might be provided by the network owner as part of the connect fee, while Stephen King could pay extra for "Yellow Pages" coverage of his works. Given directory services, the virtual library could be a direct connection between author and reader. Of course, he would also be responsible for the archiving and preservation of his novels. This could prove more difficult for an individual since most of us want our works to outlive us. Libraries offer this longevity as well as redundancy.

Publishers

Publishers offer valuable services, and some of their services probably will be needed in the virtual library of tomorrow. Publishers offer quality control of the system by deciding whose work will be allowed into the system of information distribution. They also verify the accuracy and authenticity of what they publish. And they often work with authors to improve the quality of the final product. Readers will probably continue to demand these value-added services in the virtual library; whether they will be provided by publishers as we currently know them remains to be seen. The role of reproduction and distribution currently provided by publishers is likely to disappear from the virtual library, since this function will be greatly impacted by the development of new technology. On the other hand, it is possible that publishers will take on the archival and preservation role that libraries currently play by mounting and maintaining databases of their works on the net.

A&I Services

Abstracting and indexing services currently give us valuable pointers to specialized information and enhance our ability to select the right information from the universe of information. The activities of A&I services are likely to become far more valuable as information proliferates on the net. Indeed, these services could become the providers of the directory to the virtual library; one of the key elements to its success. Those in A&I services are probably strategically positioned to become key players in the virtual library as they expand their role from indexing and abstracting to document delivery. Engineering Index is already building a file of scanned images of most of the publications they index which they intend to distribute over the Internet.

Libraries

Libraries, like publishers, play a role as gatekeepers of information. The materials they select for their collections gain a stamp of value simply by virtue of that selection. A book not selected by any library is doomed to rapid extinction. Likewise, libraries help to create the directory, both at the local and the national level, as they contribute records to the utilities. Libraries have the main responsibility of archiving society's history, culture, and learning. They have the role of assuring some equity of access to information, and they build the capital of information, in hopes of reducing the per-access cost to information. Most of what they do is supported by the government as a public good. However, under the current burden of the recession and high inflation in publishing, libraries are abandoning several of their basic missions, a trend that will undoubtedly hasten the development of the virtual library. As libraries move toward the access model, they are, in effect, abandoning their archival role and the concept of building an information capital for future users. It may be economically correct to maximize information dollars by buying only the specific information needed, but libraries are weakening their position as information providers. Libraries may also have reached the point where the archival function will need to be relegated to a few comprehensive libraries of record. For good or ill, the movement of libraries away from these basic responsibilities will accelerate the creation of the virtual library and their support as a public good could erode.

The creation of the virtual library will probably not be monolithic, nor will it follow a single model. Rather, a number of players will offer access to information in a variety of ways. A number of models are now being developed, some of which are competitive and others complementary; all, however, restructure the current system and foster new roles for the current players.

Corporation for Public Publishing Model

A CNI workshop held in Monterey, California, developed the Corporation for Public Publishing model, which proposes the establishment of a consortium of university presses to publish much of the output of university faculty via the Internet, with some funding from federal sources.[1] Each university would create a number of scholarly journals mounted on university computers and make them accessible to other member universities at no cost or low cost, much as interlibrary loan works today. This model has been put forth primarily as a response to rapidly increasing serial prices in the scientific fields of study. The CPP model would be one of distributed journals residing on numerous university computers across the world, much like the 150 or so OPACs now available. Faculty on these or other campuses would continue to serve as reviewers and editors to assure the quality of these publications. Universities would underwrite some of the costs of this model, hoping to realize savings in their library budgets.

It is assumed that university presses would take on a new role as purveyors of serials and would become more active in network activities. On campuses where university presses do not exist, the library might take on the role of fostering and administering these journals. In general, libraries are more attuned to the network environment than university presses. In the CPP model, directory services also would be distributed as they are today, and libraries would be responsible for building the national or international network directory of various journal locations resident on the net. Most likely, utilities such as OCLC would actually provide the service. Also, in this model of the virtual library, publishers would be responsible for archiving the back issues of their publications and assuring their accuracy and authenticity. Libraries have always performed the archival function, and they have the professional mindset to establish the authentication standards and services. Librarians would need to develop the editorial skills they currently do not have. One can easily imagine a new service model for librarians, who not only aid faculty in researching their publications, but also help them edit their publications.

Because of the distributed nature of this model, standards for journal access and presentation will need to be developed. The current diversity of search engines on CD-ROMs is a good example of how *not* to develop the virtual library. Imagine the need to know a different set of commands and have a different format presentation for each journal. Libraries could influence this standardization if they were the purveyors of the CPP model.

In some ways this model is already developing as faculty members begin electronic journals based in their universities and academic departments. There are well over a dozen electronic journals in existence with new ones being created almost monthly. The pioneering editors of many of these journals are strongly committed to offering these journals at no cost, and promoting a new liberal attitude toward copyright among the faculty.

At Virginia Tech, the Scholarly Communications Project was begun several years ago with the expressed intent of developing electronic journals on campus. The project now is working with faculty to publish three electronic journals, two of which had been paper-based, and one a wholly new electronic journal. A paper-based scientific journal is also being published by the project in hopes of converting it to an electronic format. Last year, this project was moved under the library administratively, to allow library faculty to develop the necessary skills to make the transition to becoming creators of the virtual library.

In the CCP model information would no longer need to be maintained in the same way. The convention of using the scholarly or scientific journal was based on the paper model of publishing. Articles were bundled together into issues for the convenience of the printer and for distribution, and journals existed to draw together scholars or scientists into the editorial process. The structure of the virtual library needs none of these conventions. The article can easily become the base unit of distribution since most of our A&I services are built on this unit. Articles can be mounted for access when ready, or even in a prepublication form when ready, thus speeding up the process of scholarly communication.

The concept of the journal might even be abandoned in the CCP model of the virtual library. Universities might instead create a database of faculty publications in all disciplines. Each department might edit its own publications, since the reputation of the department would rest on its publications' quality, and the promotion and tenure process could be wedded to the editorial process. The use of faculty files by readers of the virtual library could be tabulated, and commentary from other scholars considered as part of the reward system. Certain articles, which at some point were not considered of quality or interest, could be eliminated from the permanent archive. The reward system could be far more precise in rewarding true scholarship as the process of editing and reward are linked.

Another reason the journal format might eventually be abandoned is that the development of powerful new search engines, or "knowbots," will enable the reader to scan the content of the virtual library and bring back customized information. Our current structure of bibliography built on publishing conventions will no longer be necessary. Information will no longer have a physical location either in our libraries or with other printed material. This new structure will encourage cross-disciplinary scholarship and creativity.

National Subject Database Model

Currently many scholarly societies such as IEEE, The American Chemical Society, and the American Physical Society, are key publishers of scientific information. These publishers have shown that their pricing is reasonable, and generally they are not-for-profit organizations made up of faculty. They publish high-quality, important serials and conference proceedings which are invaluable to scientists. Drawing the work of our faculty away from these publishers does not make economic sense for the scholarly community.

The American Physical Society has done a major study of the future of their publishing enterprise, in which they envision the creation of a national or international database of physics.[2] This database would encompass all physics literature and data, drawing it together into a single database to be administered by their society. This same concept might be developed by groups in various disciplines, so that one day we would have databases for many subjects such as chemistry, agriculture, medicine, veterinary science, engineering, etc. This model could exist along side the CPP model of university-based publishing, especially in areas where there already is a strong publishing organization in existence.

The advantage of such a subject database system is that the search engines and directories could be custom designed for that discipline. A search engine that would work readily for chemistry would not be likely to work well for agriculture. Scientists in each discipline, who would be the main users of these systems, could become well versed in their use, therefore avoiding the need to rely on a library intermediary for searching the subject's main database. There would be a commonality or standardization of format, commands, etc., by database. The quality of the database would be assured because each discipline would control the information contained in the database, and the archiving of data would also be controlled by the scientists' own discipline. Librarians would be released from the need to weed their scientific collections, since the society would do so in the main database.

However, there are drawbacks to this system. It is questionable whether or not one could build an international database in specific disciplines. Will the French or Russian physicist feel comfortable knowing that the American Physical Society controls their data? Some scientists are concerned that building monolithic databases in each discipline will concentrate too much power in the hands of a few of their colleagues. New, radical ideas which depart from the accepted way of thinking may not find their way into the database. Cross-disciplinary work may not be accepted into any of these databases, depending on the purity of editors' viewpoints. This model offers very little competition within disciplines and therefore there is danger of pricing monopolies.

The librarian's role in this model will most likely be diminished, in that most scientists would do their own searching of the database, without the help of librarians. Librarians would be needed to help those outside of the specific discipline who wish to investigate new areas, or those whose interests are cross disciplinary. This would be especially true for undergraduates who study in many areas.

The National Utility Model

In the creation of the virtual library, directory services will be a major factor in making it a success, since locating information will be the key element, and far more important than owning information. National utilities like OCLC or RLG already perform these services at the bibliographic and holdings level. In the virtual library, the indexes will need to be at least at the article level, and eventually at the concept level. OCLC already works with many international libraries, another key component in creating a true virtual library. The utilities already have sophisticated billing systems in place which will be a strategic element for success. OCLC, unlike any of the other players, has invested considerable research and development into creating an electronic journal in partnership with AAAS. OCLC also has a state-of-the-art telecommunication and computer system in place.

In this national utility model, a utility like OCLC could form partnerships with various publishers in which the utility would create the directory to their publications, distribute them over their network or via the Internet, bill for their usage, and archive the back files. The editorial and quality control functions would still reside with the publishers, as would the copyright. This model builds on the current structure and leaves most of the current players in the position of offering their current services. Many publishers already depend somewhat on others, such as Faxon, for distribution and billing, so the move to cooperate with an organization like OCLC is not out of the question. What does not exist is a history of cooperation and trust between the library community and publishers, and this has been exacerbated recently by the rapid rise of serials prices. The fact that the utilities are governed by librarians will make alliances between utilities and publishers more difficult to develop.

Under this model, librarians initially would continue to play an important role in the accessing of information, since the utilities do not have ready access to readers or users. Subscriptions to these electronic publications probably will still be through libraries rather than individuals. Librarians, by controlling the governance of the utilities, will have greater control of the standardization of search engines, the presentation, and the archiving of information. On the other hand, almost any model of the virtual library will diminish the traditional role of librarians by vending information directly to the end-user and therefore, organizations like OCLC will have significant problems convincing their governance structures that they should move aggressively in directions that erode the traditional position of librarians.

Distributed For-Profit Model

Under the Distributed For-Profit model, a variety of publishers, and jobbers like Faxon or EBSCO, would begin to create full-text databases. It is unlikely that publishers by themselves will begin moving in this direction since they do not have the infrastructure of computer systems, customer billing systems, or access to the Internet. They also currently do not have any directories comprehensive enough to appeal to their clients. Therefore, it is very likely that publishers will turn to their current jobbers to create the necessary functions that will make the virtual library a reality. The current jobbers already handle billing and some distribution for the publishers and a few, like Faxon, are busily developing directory services at the article level. (It is interesting to note that Faxon, a jobber, and OCLC, a directory provider, like CARL and EBSCO have a joint relationship to offer document delivery services. Faxon is also working with libraries to supply the actual documents.) Currently this development is aimed at document delivery services, but the natural progression is to the virtual library. These jobbers have an advantage in that they currently supply subscriptions to the business and professional community as well as academic. The jobbers have a further advantage in that they have developed trust relationships with publishers and with libraries, where other players have not.

Another alternative could be that some of the current abstracting and indexing services will link their services to the actual full-text file in cooperation with the publisher. Engineering Index is ready to offer a document delivery service for the 2,400 publications in engineering that it indexes. They have agreements with some of the engineering publishers to scan and store their publications and deliver them via the Internet. It would seem obvious that the next step would be to get the electronic full-text file directly from the publisher. Indeed, Elsevier is allowing EI access to the scanned images of their materials science journals as part of their TULIP project, which will investigate economic models for distributing scanned images of their publications directly to universities. The A&I services are in a good strategic position, in that directories will provide the key access to the virtual library. The A&I services segment the literature according to user groups, and in many cases they currently market their services directly to the end-users who have been using them in an online environment for years. In many ways this possibility closely parallels the model of the scholarly society creating subject-based databases. A cooperative agreement between the scholarly societies and the specific A&I services in that discipline might be a powerful force in creating the virtual library.

An even more powerful cooperative arrangement might exist between the publishers, the A&I services, and the "baby bells." Immense amounts of venture capital would be available, and the baby bells could offer the telecommunications and billing systems that the other two lack. Bringing the baby bells into the picture would also quicken the pace of making the virtual library ubiquitous and available in every home world-wide. One of the major drawbacks of a virtual library linked to the Internet is its limited distribution to select academic sites. The baby bells would solve this problem and offer the wider possibility of making the virtual library a multi-media database. Publishers and libraries fear their entry into this arena; however, a coalition of these players could make the virtual library a reality much sooner.

It is also a possibility that various publishers might develop cooperative relationships with universities for mounting the full-text files of their publications on the university's computer to be distributed via the Internet. Although this possibility has some advantages, most universities have no method of billing for use, and the directory services would need to be offered in much the same way as it is done by the utilities. Libraries at these universities could catalog the files and enter them into the national databases. This possibility would offer a combined model, somewhere between an entirely private system and the model first discussed, the Corporation for Public Publishing. Publishers could continue their role as editors and reviewers, and providers of venture capital, while universities could provide distribution, archiving, and directory services. In this model, new licensing or copyright agreements might develop which would be advantageous to both parties since there would be a shared investment in producing the virtual library.

Under this model of private sector control of much of the virtual library, the issue of archiving the scholarly record becomes critical. Currently much of this cost is borne by libraries which are funded as part of the public good. Private investors may not be willing to bear the cost of archiving in the virtual library data which is not in demand. Public information policy will need to be developed that mandates the continuation of the archival function once a private information provider no longer wishes to maintain a specific file. In a multinational, distributed environment this could prove very difficult. Of course, there is no available data today on how much information is lost in our current distributed print system due to no one maintaining back files.

Information Structure

John Garrett and Joseph Alen have proposed an interesting structure for information in the virtual library or, as they call it, the digital library.[3] They envision the construction of various databases, based on factors such as authenticity, subject, and format. For instance, the virtual library might have a significant database of what is today known as "bulletin board information," which would be free or very low cost. This type of information would not be authenticated; in other words, no one would verify the author or whether the text was as the author had originally written it. No one would have checked the information for errors, and updating could not be relied on. Access might be by crude search engines and the information might or might not be included in official directories. In library parlance, this type of database could be considered as ephemeral material.

Other databases envisioned by Garrett and Alen, would be what they call the "Quality Management Database" and the "On-line Scientific Library." Each of these databases would contain information which has been authenticated, updated for currency and correctness, with high-quality search engines and directories. These databases would have an elaborate mechanism for royalty payments and assurances that one could legally use the information contained in the database and that authors and rights holders would be protected against unauthorized use.

A third type of database would be the "photo archive," where stored images could be selected by users for incorporation into derivative works.

Obviously, this type of media database takes us well beyond the simple concept of full-text to the virtual library of sound and video. These multi-media databases will allow the user to tailor new information products. In addition to containing the information packages of today—the article, monograph, film, or music score—the virtual library may contain more basic information units that are accessed by "knowbots" or intelligent agents and used to create custom information packages for the user. In this new information world, the line between author, creator, and user may well blur or vanish, in that users of the virtual library will be able to create their own derivative works with ease. Before "knowbots" with sophisticated capability are developed, the role of librarians may change from developing collections and helping users access these collections to a new role of creating specific information packages to meet individual user needs.

Already, government information is increasingly available in electronic form only. This data ranges from full-text to statistical and numeric data of interest to a diverse audience. Some is available through dial-up access while other data is produced on CD-ROM, but as raw data or with limited search engines. Secondary providers then add value to this data by creating user-friendly access to it. We may find that the same data will exist in many forms in the virtual library, with differing search engines and differing updates at different prices. Clifford Lynch sees the day when the price of information could differ according to presentation and the price could change rapidly according to demand.[4] Articles by a new Nobel Prize winner could suddenly increase in cost with his or her fame. Instead of having journals priced for the year, the cost of access could change overnight as the value of the dollar rises and falls. Information might even appear in the futures market, where acquisitions librarians could buy a thousand articles from the scientific database when the price is low to avoid higher prices in the future.

Conclusion

The development of the virtual library will undoubtedly follow many of the scenarios listed above as it evolves over the next decade. Some of these arrangements are already underway, as Elsevier works with a number of universities in the TULIP project, OCLC and Faxon cooperate to create "Faxon Express," and EI plans to deliver scanned images of the publications they index. These are as yet small beginnings; however, as has been the case with CD-ROM, developments in the information field can be very fast-moving, with significant impact on library services and budgets. The telecommunications infrastructure needed to support the virtual library is rapidly being put into place, and the current economic climate will foster change as our current system becomes untenable.

Dangers lie ahead as the virtual library evolves. The redundancy of the current system of local library collections and OPACs linked to the national utilities offers safeguards of our cultural and scholarly heritage and assures that they will be preserved. Our system of publicly supported libraries safeguards equitable access to information, while the publishers assure the authenticity and quality of information. As the virtual library evolves, economics and individual needs will likely drive the system, and public information policy may not keep up with its development.

As the virtual library evolution takes place, certain elements must be assured. They are: that information be presented in a standardized format; that distribution and access be ubiquitous and international; that powerful and standardized search engines be created and maintained; that the accuracy and authenticity of information be assured; that the intellectual property rights of creators and rights holders be safeguarded; and that the scholarly and cultural record be preserved. The role of librarians is critical in assuring that these standards and safeguards are developed in the virtual library.

Safeguarding the archival function now performed by libraries will be especially crucial in a virtual library environment which is likely to be commercial. A possible solution could be to designate the Library of Congress as the repository of the "National Digital Archive." There is the strong likelihood that information units will be removed from the virtual library once they are no longer economically viable. If we go by the 80/20 rule—that twenty percent of our collections amount to 80 percent of our use—then significant portions of the virtual library will not be used, or used so rarely that the cost of maintaining them will be questionable. Copyright could be restructured so that it expires on any information unit once it is removed from the virtual library by the rights holder. At that point it could be transferred to the "National Digital Archive" for permanent storage and free use by anyone. The Library of Congress would then be responsible for refreshing the data, maintaining it in a useable form, and making it available to users. Information in the "National Digital Archive" may not be immediately available or searchable to the same degree as in the virtual library. The ADONIS project may serve as another model for archiving the scholarly record. Storage of little used information on CD-ROM may be a very cost-effective method and relatively stable. (The debate on the stability of CD-ROM as a preservation medium continues; however, we can assume advances will be made in storage mediums such as CD-ROM.) The ADONIS project also offers an alternative method of distributing electronic information to less-developed countries which do not have an advanced telecommunications infrastructure.

There has been much discussion about the impact of the virtual library on copyright and visa versa. Increasingly, information will not be seen as property or a commodity, but as an event or service.[5] The more we perceive it as such, the less copyright will be an issue. As the role of each player in the information world changes, new means of compensation for their services will evolve. Compensation, not protection, will become the basis of our thinking.

The role of librarians will likely diminish as the new order is created and local collections become less important. Acquisition and cataloging functions will be limited to a fraction of what they are today. Building local library collections may become a thing of the past, but librarians increasingly will be needed to help library patrons navigate the new world of information. Information users will need to be taught a new set of skills to use the virtual library and many will need librarians to mediate their information needs. Hopefully, universities will be active players in creating the virtual library by supporting those pioneering faculty who are already producing electronic journals. If they do, librarians, in concert with the faculty, could broaden their skills to become part of the process of creating information, as well as being purveyors of information. The Knowledge Management project under Richard Lucier at Johns Hopkins, where the Human Genome Project is underway, can be a model for librarians' involvement in the process of knowledge creation. Although this project may not easily be replicated in other fields, the model still has relevance to the future of our profession.

Librarians all are aware of "information overload" or the term "drinking from a firehose." Filtering or refining information will become an increasingly important value-added service to individuals who have neither the time nor the skills to find the information they need. Librarians are better suited to this role than any other group. They need to define and refine these skills as the electronic information world develops. They need to be creators of this world, but most of all they need to impart their values to this world, preserving the legacy of humankind, assuring equitable access to information, and serving the needs of information users.

Notes

1. Chet Grycz, "Electronic Scholarly Publishing," *DLA Bulletin* 11:1.
2. Report of the Task Force on Electronic Information Systems, *Bulletin of the American Physical Society*, 36:4 (1991), 1119.
3. John R. Garrett and Joseph S. Alen, "Toward a Copyright Management System for Digital Libraries," *Copyright Clearance Center* (1991).
4. Clifford Lynch, speech given at Sweet Briar College, Sweet Briar, Virginia, November 12, 1991.
5. Robert Kost, "Technology Giveth . . . ," *Serials Review,* Vol. 18 No. 1/2 (January 1992): 54-58.

Index

Contributors

Joanne R. Euster is Vice President for University Libraries at Rutgers University in New Brunswick, NJ.

Paul M. Gherman is Special Assistant to the Vice President for Information Systems at the Virginia Polytechnic Institute and State University in Blacksburg.

Charles B. Lowry is Director of Libraries at the University of Texas at Arlington.

Theresa Maylone is Adjunct Professor at the Palmer School of Library and Information Science, at the C.W. Post Campus of Long Island University, Brookville, NY.

James I. Penrod is Vice President for Information Resources Management at California State University at Los Angeles.

Gary M. Pitkin is Dean of University Libraries at the University of Northern Colorado in Greely.

Jane Norman Ryland is President of CAUSE — The Association for the Management of Information Technology in Higher Education, located in Boulder, CO.

Anne Woodsworth is Dean of the Palmer School of Library and Information Science, at the C.W. Post Campus of Long Island University, Brookville, NY.